Take your Best Shot
The Illustrated Beginner's Guide to Digital Photography

Kevin Wilson

Take your Best Shot

Publisher: Elluminet Press
Director: Kevin Wilson
Lead Editor: Steven Ashmore
Technical Reviewer: Mike Taylor, Robert Ashcroft
Copy Editors: Joanne Taylor, James Marsh
Proof Reader: Robert Price
Indexer: James Marsh
Cover Designer: Kevin Wilson

eBook versions and licenses are also available for most titles. Any source code or other supplementary materials referenced by the author in this text is available to readers at

www.elluminetpress.com/resources

For detailed information about how to locate your book's resources, go to

www.elluminetpress.com/resources

Table of Contents

About the Author

With over 20 years' experience in the computer industry, Kevin Wilson has made a career out of technology and showing others how to use it. After earning a master's degree in computer science, software engineering, and multimedia systems, Kevin has held various positions in the IT industry including graphic & web design, programming, building & managing corporate networks, and IT support.

He serves as senior writer and director at Elluminet Press Ltd, he periodically teaches computer science at college, and works as an IT trainer in England while researching for his PhD. His books have become a valuable resource among the students in England, South Africa, Canada, and in the United States.

Kevin's motto is clear: "If you can't explain something simply, then you haven't understood it well enough." To that end, he has created the Exploring Tech Computing series, in which he breaks down complex technological subjects into smaller, easy-to-follow steps that students and ordinary computer users can put into practice.

Acknowledgements

Thanks to all the staff at Luminescent Media & Elluminet Press for their passion, dedication and hard work in the preparation and production of this book.

To all my friends and family for their continued support and encouragement in all my writing projects.

To all my colleagues, students and testers who took the time to test procedures and offer feedback on the book.

Finally thanks to you the reader for choosing this book. I hope it helps you take better photos and enjoy photography as much as we do.

Digital Cameras

Since the 1990s, digital cameras have become more and more common, and more affordable. Because of this, it's easy to get started with photography and you don't need to buy a professional camera to get good results.

There are various different types of cameras on the market, from full size SLRs to compact point and shoot.

In this chapter, we'll take a look at

- How a Digital Camera Works
- Crop and Full Frame Sensors
- Storage
- Image Formats
- Digital SLR Cameras
- Mirrorless Cameras
- Bridge Cameras
- Compact Point-and-Shoot
- Smart Phone Camera

Lets take a look at the basics of how a digital camera works, some of the different types of cameras on the market.

How a Digital Camera Works

In principal, a digital camera is similar to a traditional film-based camera. There's a viewfinder to aim and frame your shot, a lens to focus the image onto a light sensor, and some means of storage.

Optics

In a tradition film based camera, light-sensitive film captures images and is used to store them after chemical development. Digital photography uses a combination of an image sensor and memory storage, which allows images to be captured in a digital format that is available instantly with no need for a film development process.

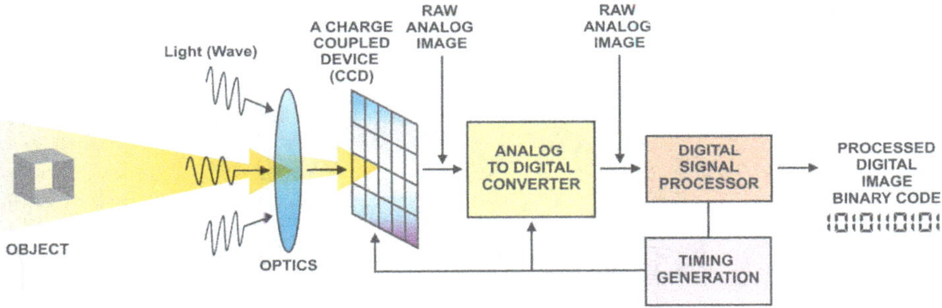

Although the principle may be the same as a film camera, the inner workings of a digital camera are a little different. Instead of film, a sensor called a charge coupled device (CCD) or sometimes CMOS (complementary metal-oxide semiconductor) is used.

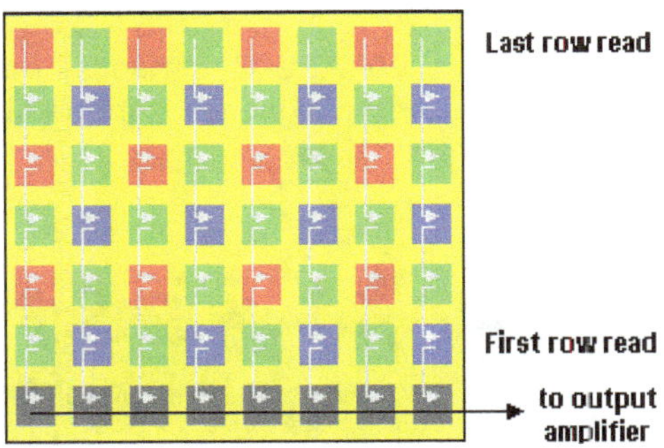

Each sensor element converts light into a voltage proportional to the brightness which is passed into an analogue-to-digital converter (ADC). This converts the fluctuations of the CCD into a discrete binary code. The brighter the light, the higher the voltage and the brighter the resulting pixel. The more elements, the higher the resolution, and the greater the detail that can be captured.

The output from the ADC is sent to a digital signal processor (DSP) which adjusts contrast and detail. It then compresses the data and stores it as an image on the storage medium (such as an SD memory card).

The CCD or CMOS sensors are fixed in place and it can go on taking photos for the lifetime of the camera. There's no need to wind film between two spools either, which helps minimize the number of moving parts.

Crop and Full Frame Sensors

A full frame sensor is 35mm by 24mm in size and tends to offer the best image quality.

Crop sensors, sometimes called APS-C sensors, are much smaller. They are not all exactly the same physical size, as this depends on the manufacturer. Anything smaller than 35mm x 24mm is a crop sensor.

The main difference between a full frame and crop sensor is the field of view. The focal lengths marked on lenses are based on the 35mm standard.

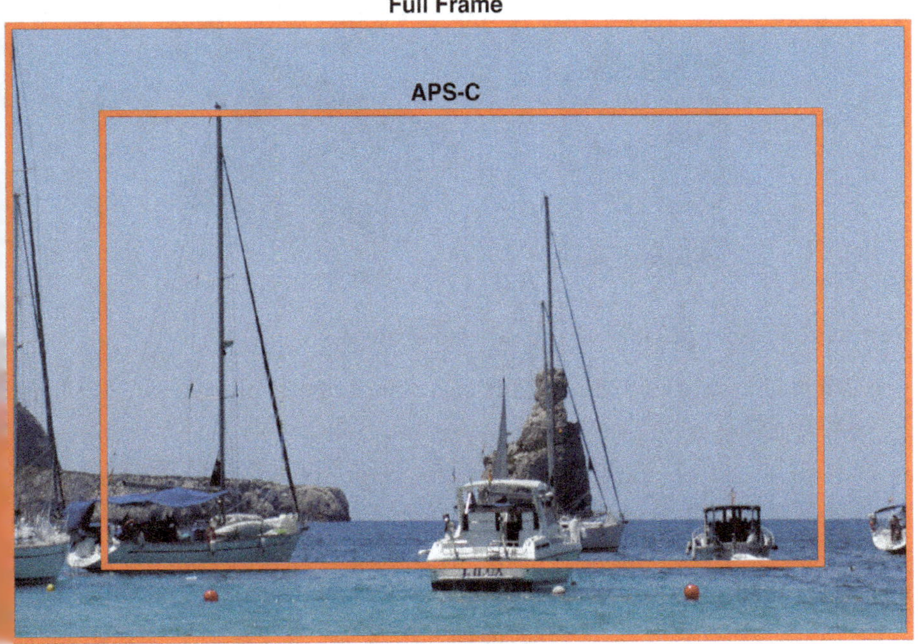

So, if you are using a crop sensor, you're cropping out the edges of the frame which effectively increases the focal length.

Nikon APS-C sensors have a 1.5x crop factor, while Canons have a 1.6x crop factor. This means with any lens you attach, you need to multiply the focal length on the side of the lens by the crop factor.

If you were to use a lens that is 50mm, on a crop sensor you'd need to multiply this by the crop factor. So on a Canon it would be equivalent to an 80mm lens on a full frame camera.

Full frame sensors are better low light with high ISO, resulting in a better quality, cleaner image than with a crop sensor.

Full frame sensors make better architectural and landscape photography solutions due to having a wider angle of view. Full frame cameras also provide a broader dynamic range which can help when taking photos of scenes with both deep shadows and bright highlights.

Depth of field is a lot shallower on a full frame camera, which gives more artistic control.

Storage

Modern digital cameras use removable storage. This is usually an SD card, Compact Flash, or sometimes CFast. The photographs are saved to the card as an image file - usually JPG or RAW.

Removable storage offer two main advantages:

- Once a memory card is full it can simply be removed and replaced by another.

- Given the necessary PC hardware, memory cards can be inserted directly into a PC to transfer the photos.

The most common memory card is the SD Card. This can be a full sized SD card, or a Micro SD card.

Standard SD cards are commonly used in digital cameras, and many laptops have standard size SD card readers built in. Tablets, phones and small cameras usually use micro SD cards.

You can get an SD Card adapter if your SD card reader does not read Micro SD cards.

There are various types of SD cards available, each are marked with a speed classification symbol indicating the data transfer speed. If you are using a digital camera to shoot high resolution photos or videos, the faster the data transfer speeds the better. You'll want at least 80Mbps or faster. You can see a summary in the table below.

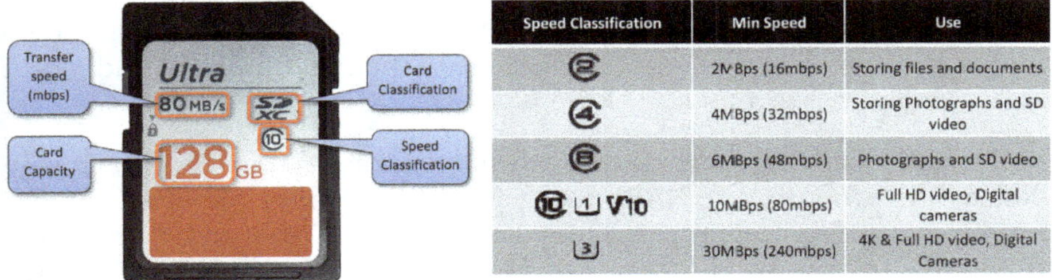

Speed Classification	Min Speed	Use
C2	2MBps (16mbps)	Storing files and documents
C4	4MBps (32mbps)	Storing Photographs and SD video
C6	6MBps (48mbps)	Photographs and SD video
U1 V10	10MBps (80mbps)	Full HD video, Digital cameras
3	30MBps (240mbps)	4K & Full HD video, Digital Cameras

SDHC stands for "Secure Digital High Capacity", and supports capacities up to 32 GB.

SDXC stands for "Secure Digital eXtended Capacity", and supports capacities up to 2 TB.

SDUC stands for "Secure Digital Ultra Capacity", and supports capacities up to 128 TB.

Avoid the cheap SD cards, as they usually have slow data transfer rates. You'll need a high data transfer rate when shooting in RAW format, or recording video.

Card readers are available for all the common media types – CompactFlash, SmartMedia, MemoryStick, SD Card etc.

These card readers plug in to a USB port on a computer using a USB cable, allowing you to read the memory card as if it were an external hard disk for flash drive.

You can then transfer the photos to your computer for long term storage, editing or printing.

Image Formats

Most digital cameras store photos in JPG format, however some cameras also offer RAW and TIFF formats.

When you press the shutter button on the camera, the data picked up by the sensor is processed. The contrast, brightness, white balance and saturation settings is set, the image is then compressed and saved on the memory card as a JPG file.

A RAW file isn't processed and is just the raw data from the image sensor. As a result, the RAW image is a much larger file but contains all the data from the sensor. This allows you to tweak and manipulate the image in post production using Photoshop Camera RAW or Adobe Lightroom. You can brighten shadows, darken skies, change the white balance, contrast. These apps come with a Creative Cloud Subscription from Adobe.

You can also use free alternatives such as Microsoft Photos App with the RAW image extension, and Google Photos in Windows, or the Photos App on a Mac.

Some cameras also offer the chance to leave your photos uncompressed. These images are saved as a TIFF file. Note that TIFF files are usually massive in size which means you won't get many photos on your memory card.

I always shoot in RAW format which allows me greater control over the photograph in post production. However, if you don't intend to adjust the photos later on and simply want to post them on social media or send to friends, shooting in JPG might be a better option.

Digital SLR (or DSLR)

These cameras tend to be expensive, with high quality interchangeable lenses for different shots with full manual controls of all the settings. These cameras also tend to be quite big and bulky and are designed to be used in professional studios and professional photographers.

These cameras are known as a single lens reflex because what you see through the view finder is what the sensor will see through the lens. In other words, you see the shot you're going to take.

These cameras have a wide range of difference lenses, such as wide angle, portrait, prime, macro lenses, as well as large zoom lenses.

Chapter 1: Digital Cameras

When you look through the view finder, the light from the lens bounces off the mirror, through a pentaprism and into the view finder. This is how you see what you're shooting through the lens.

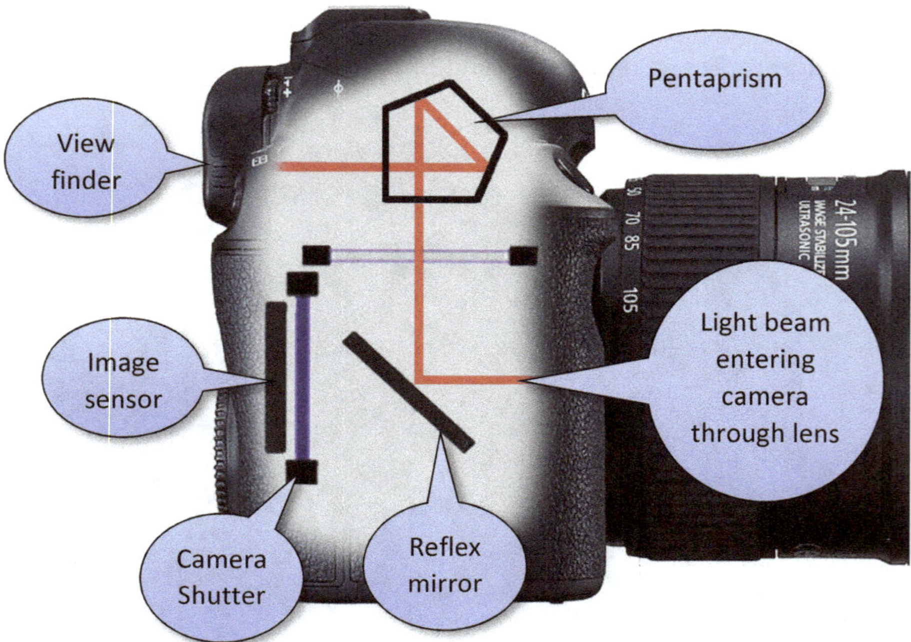

When you take the photo, the mirror snaps out of the way and the shutter opens, exposing the light to the image sensor.

Mirrorless Cameras

Mirrorless cameras don't use an optical viewfinder. Instead, the imaging sensor is exposed to the light coming through the lens at all times. As a result, you get a digital preview of the photo you're about to take either on the rear LCD screen or an electronic viewfinder (EVF).

The advantage of an EVF is that the camera can overlay extra information such as what's in focus or under/overexposed, and you get an accurate preview of the depth of field and exposure.

One disadvantage is, the refresh rate of the live image in the EVF lags a bit, and can sometimes cause a delay meaning you miss some fast actions.

These cameras also have interchangeable lenses but are a lot smaller and compact than their SLR equivalents.

These make a great alternative to full sized SLR cameras.

Bridge Cameras

Bridge cameras were designed to fill the gap between full SLR cameras and consumer point & shoot.

These cameras are much like the SLRs but are a cut down version and don't usually have interchangeable lenses. The lenses often offer a wide zoom range such as 50x, with apertures of around 4.8-5.6 f, which are much slower than many SLR lenses.

These cameras are a bit smaller than SLRs but are still quite bulky and great for a hobbyist with a good knowledge of photography, who love taking a lot of photographs.

These cameras also feature full manual controls over aperture, shutter and ISO, allowing for more creativity, as well as automated controls for general point and shoot.

Bridge cameras make a good starting point for those who want to get more serious about photography on a small budget. However, entry level SLR or mirrorless cameras offer more versatility and options.

Compact Point-and-Shoot

Somewhat being slowly replaced by smart phone cameras. These cameras are aimed at consumers and tend to be quite small and compact, easy to fit in your pocket or take on holiday/vacation with you.

The lenses are fixed on most models and most of the camera settings are applied automatically, which usually suite most ordinary users.

These cameras usually lack a view finder in favour of an LCD screen on the back. This tends to make these cameras a bit slow for any serious photography.

Smart Phone Camera

This is probably the most commonly found digital camera in the world. The quality of these cameras has progressed considerably in the past few years but still doesn't quite rival DSLRs with picture quality.

You can also buy add on lenses for most smart phones. These are small external lenses that clip over the built in lens on your phone. Many of these lenses are universal meaning they will fit any phone.

There are various types of lenses you can add.

Telephoto lenses capture distant objects without using the digital zoom on your camera.

Wide angle lenses enhance the angle of view of your smartphone camera, so you can take a wider angle from closer range.

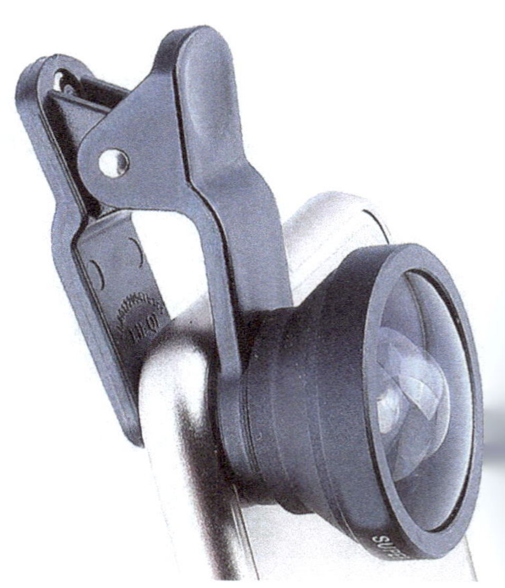

Macro lenses capture close up objects in detail.

Fisheye lenses create creative shots with extreme wide angle views.

Some Points to Consider

There are a lot of cameras you can buy for about £100 and they are usually fine for simple point and shoot and have some pretty good features. Some of the more expensive models have more control over the settings, larger zoom lenses and more capacity.

When choosing your camera ask yourself what kind of shooting do you want to do.

Are you mainly going to be taking snapshots of your friends and family?

For snapshots, almost any digital camera will do and most of them are pretty well featured now days. For more artistic photos, look for a camera with a larger lens and one that gives you more manual control.

What about portability? If you want a camera that you can easily put in your pocket, look for a slim, light camera.

Do you want to take more artistic photographs? DSLRs and bridge cameras give you more options and flexibility here.

With larger cameras, such as DSLRs and Bridge, you may need to carry them in a shoulder bag, which makes them less portable.

Perhaps a mirrorless camera. These offer similar functionality as a full sized SLR but are a lot smaller and more portable.

What about zoom lenses? A typical point-and-shoot camera may have a 5x optical zoom, which is good for most purposes and I would suggest that as minimum.

Some cameras have much more powerful zooms up to 35x. The extra zoom can really come in handy for sports, holiday/vacation photos, wildlife, or any situation where you want to get close to the action.

Is my smart phone camera good enough for what I want?

Exploring your Camera

There are many different types of cameras and they all have slightly different buttons and settings, so I will do my best to try to explain some of the main features found on most cameras.

In this chapter we'll take a look at

- LCD Panels & Menus
- Dials and Buttons
- Optical vs Digital Zoom
- Macro Modes
- Light Metering Modes
- Shooting Modes
- White Balance
- Expose Compensation
- Time Lapse
- Slomo
- Filters & Effects
- Panoramic
- Timers
- Image Stabilizers
- Storage

LCD Panels & Menus

A colour LCD panel is a feature that is present on virtually all modern digital cameras. It acts as a mini GUI (or graphic user interface), allowing the user to adjust the full range of settings offered by the camera. Here's the LCD panel on the Canon 6D.

The LCD can also be an invaluable aid to previewing photos you've just taken, as well as organising and arranging photos without needing to connect to a PC. You can view a particular image full-screen, zoom in close and, if required, delete it from the memory card.

Some digital cameras allow the LCD to be used for composition instead of the viewfinder.

On some models this is hidden on the rear of a hinged flap that has to be folded out, rotated and then folded back into place. Here, on the Canon 60D, the screen flips out from a panel on the back of the camera.

On the face of it this is a little cumbersome – but it has a couple of advantages over a fixed screen. First, the screen is protected when not in use and, second, it can be flexibly positioned so as to allow the photographer to take a self-portrait or to hold the camera above their head whilst still retaining control over the framing of the shot.

Compact Cameras

Most compact cameras have various dials and buttons that allow you to change the settings and navigate the menus on the LCD screen.

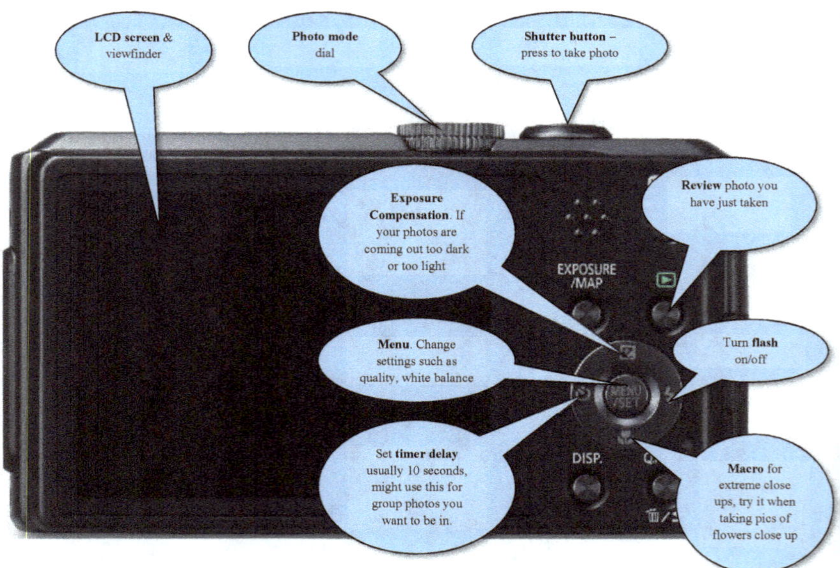

Along the top, you'll usually see a dial that allows you to change the shooting mode (auto, manual, shutter/aperture priority etc), as well as the shutter button to take the photo. On some compact cameras, you'll also see a zoom lever, but on most SLR and higher end cameras you adjust the zoom and focus on the actual lens itself.

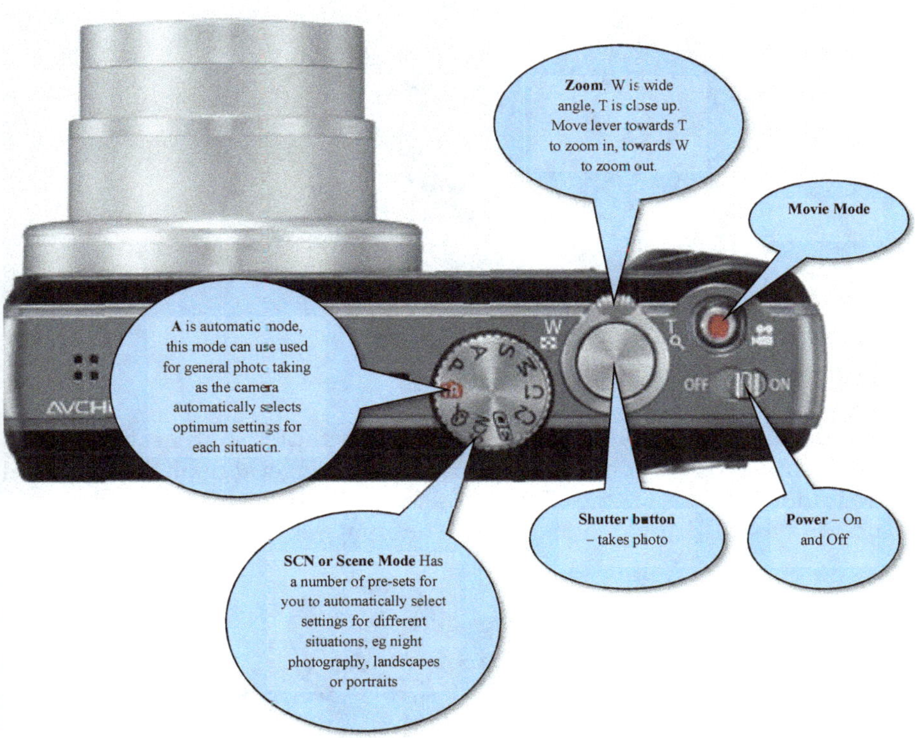

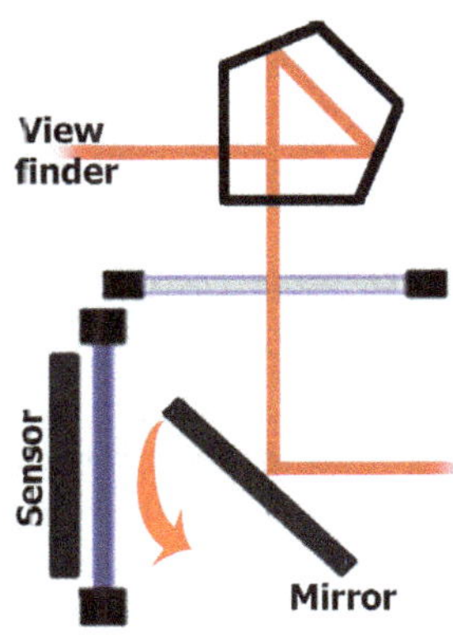

SLR Cameras

SLR cameras are designed a little bit differently. A single-lens reflex camera (SLR) is a camera that uses a mirror and penta-prism system to reflect the light coming through the lens up to the view finder. This allows the photographer to see through the lens meaning you get an exact view of what is going to be captured. When you press the shutter button to take the photo, the mirror flips out of the way, allowing light to pass through to the sensor. This is why the view finder goes momentarily dark while the photo is being taken.

Here is the Canon 6D SLR camera.

Mirrorless Cameras

A mirrorless camera is mechanically much simpler than an SLR. Light passes through the lens directly onto the image sensor. The optical view finder found in the SLR is replaced with an electronic viewfinder which is basically a video feed from the image sensor.

This offers an advantage over the SLR, as the image seen in the viewfinder will show the white balance, contrast, brightness and saturation of the image you're about to take. In addition, information including live histograms can be placed within the viewfinder, allowing the photographer to see exactly what they are shooting and how the photo will look. Here in the photo above, is the Sony A7 mirrorless camera. Most mirrorless cameras are thinner and lighter than SLRs.

Optical vs Digital Zoom

Digital cameras offer two distinct varieties of zoom feature: optical zoom and digital zoom.

Optical zoom works in much the same way as a zoom lens on a traditional camera. Produced by the lens system, it is the magnification difference between minimum and maximum focal lengths. Importantly, in digital cameras this magnification occurs before an image is recorded in pixels.

Digital zoom, on the other hand, is arguably little more than a marketing gimmick. With digital zoom, the image is enlarged by the camera's software, then cropped to give the illusion that the image has been zoomed in. The downside to this process is the loss of resolution.

When an image that has been digitally zoomed 2x is printed, it will effectively be viewed at half its original resolution.

A more sophisticated from of digital zoom uses the digital camera's software to interpolate the cropped image back to its original resolution. In this method, fewer of the original pixels are used to represent the enlarged image, which will appear less sharp as a result. Some digital cameras provide a digital zoom feature as an alternative to an true optical zoom, others provide it as an additional feature.

Macro Modes

For close-up work, a macro function is often provided on most compact cameras, allowing photos to be taken at a distance as close as 3cm but more typically supporting a focal range of around 10-50cm. On an SLR camera, this is usually achieved by attaching a macro lens.

Light Metering Modes

Every digital camera has a fully automatic mode metering that allows a user to simply point and shoot. However, they also offer several different ways of controlling the exposure of an image. A good exposure will result in an image that has balanced contrast and brightness, with no areas that are too bright and washed out or too dark which also creates loss of detail.

Center weighted metering is the system used by many digital cameras to measure the correct exposure. With this system, the camera measures the amount of light mostly around the centre area of the lens and less towards the edges.

For many situations this works well, but in some lighting situations, centre weighted metering can produce poorly exposed photos. If the scene to be photographed has light areas and dark areas, for example in the shade of trees on bright sunny days with lots of sunlight and shadowed areas, centre weighed metering will often either overexpose the bright sections, or underexpose the dark sections.

Some digital cameras offer matrix type metering systems, which break the scene into several areas and measures each individual area's exposure. This results in an image with a balanced exposure throughout.

Spot metering is another option included on some digital camera models. This measures the exposure at a small, precise portion in the centre of the lens, allowing the user to ensure perfect exposure on a particular section of the scene.

Shooting Modes

Programmed auto-exposure modes (P) keep the basic exposure settings automatic while providing manual access to other camera settings. Some offer aperture (Av) and shutter priority (Tv) modes which allow the user to set the f-stop or shutter speed, and then automatically calculate the other settings needed to expose an image correctly. These are usually selected using a dial on the top of the camera, or in the menu system on the LCD display.

Some cameras provide a manual exposure mode (M), allowing the photographer plenty of artistic licence. Typically, three parameters are set in this mode: f-stops, shutter speed and ISO. Other settings can also be adjusted such as white balance, exposure compensation, and flash.

Other Features

Many digital cameras offer other settings such as white balance, exposure compensation, self timer, panoramic modes, video recording and so on.

White Balance

Different types of light (outdoor, fluorescent, and so on) will have an impact on the colours in images. White balance provides a means to correct for the effect of the lighting conditions, such as sunny, cloudy, incandescent or fluorescent.

Exposure Compensation

Exposure compensation alters the overall exposure of the shot relative to the metered ideal exposure. This feature is similar to that a SLR cameras, allowing a shot to be intentionally under- or over-exposed to achieve a particular effect. A flash power setting allows the strength of the flash to be incrementally altered and a flash sync setting allows use of the flash to be forced, regardless of the camera's other settings.

Some cameras offer what is referred to as automatic exposure bracketing. With this, several frames are shot when the shutter is released, each at a different exposure setting. The exposure that gave the best result can then be selected.

Burst Mode

Most digital cameras offer a number of image exposure timing options. One of the most popular is a burst mode that allows a number of shots to be taken with a single press of the shutter. The speed and number of sequential shots that can be captured in a burst is dependent on the amount of internal memory the camera possesses, the image size selected and the degree of compression applied to the photos. Cameras with fast burst rates – specified as a fps rate – generally have a large amount of buffer memory, which is used as a temporarily store prior an image being processed and written to the camera's primary image storage medium.

Time Lapse

Some compact cameras, and phone cameras offer this feature. Time lapse delays multi-picture capture over a preselected interval, this gives the impression of speeding up a scene.

Slomo

Slow motion video, takes video at a high frame rate, such as 120 or 240 frames per second. This is played back at the normal 25 frames per second, and gives the impression of slowing down the action.

Filters & Effects

On some compact cameras and phone cameras, you have the option to select between various effects and electronic filters such as monochrome, negative and sepia modes. You can also add filters to warm up an image, bring out various colours and so on.

Panoramic

Some compact cameras and phone cameras add a panoramic mode which allows you to create panoramic photos. This is often achieved by capturing a series of images and then stitching them into a single panoramic landscape using special-purpose software.

Timers

A self-timer is a common feature, typically providing a 3 or 10-second delay between the time the shutter is pressed and when the picture is taken.   Use the 3-second delay for the situations where you don't need to be in the shot, or in situations where you have the camera in a position where you can't reach the shutter button - eg high up on a monopod. Also useful for night shots, as this avoids camera shake caused by pressing the shutter button. Use the 10-second delay you're taking a group shot, and you want in it. The 10 second delay gives you some extra time to start the timer, then get back to the group comfortably.

Image Stabilizers

Some digital cameras feature image stabilisation systems. This is particularly useful when used in conjunction with high powered zoom lenses, when it can be very difficult to keep the camera still enough to create a clear image. Image stabilizers are useful in low light situations when using a slow shutter speed.

Storage

Higher-end cameras provide support for two memory cards and features more commonly associated with SLR cameras. Here on the Canon 5D Mark III, you can see slots for two different memory cards.

This is particularly useful on professional level cameras and allows you to save a backup of your photos to another card, in case the card you're using gets damaged or the photos corrupted.

3 Lenses

A camera lens is actually several lenses combined into one unit. A single converging lens could form a real image on the film, but it would be warped by a number of aberrations.

One of the most significant warping factors is that different colours of light bend differently when moving through a lens. This is called chromatic aberration and produces an image where the colours are not lined up correctly.

In this section, we'll take a look at

- Lens Basics
- Focal Length
- Prime Lenses
- Zoom/Telephoto Lenses
- Macro Lenses
- Fisheye Lenses

Let's start with lens basics.

Lens Basics

Lenses are made from either glass or plastic. Camera lenses are compound lenses, meaning they are constructed using various different individual lenses to increase sharpness and reduce distortions and aberrations.

Focal Length

The focal length of a lens is the distance between the lens itself and the image sensor when in focus.

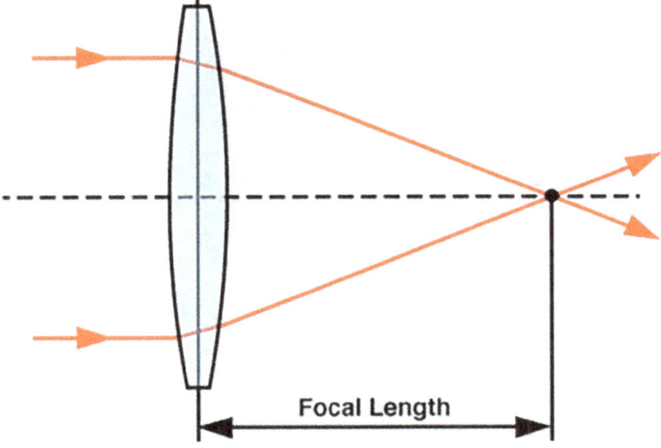

The focal length of any camera lens is measured in millimetres (mm) and is marked on the side of the lens casing.

The shorter the focal length, the wider the angle of view (eg 45mm). To zoom in you lengthen the focal length (eg 150mm).

Types of Lenses

There are various types of lenses to choose from. You will find prime lenses, zoom lenses, as well as special lenses such as macro and fisheye.

Prime Lens

With a prime lens, the focal length is fixed and they usually have a maximum aperture of f2.8 or f1.2. These lenses offer a much sharper image than a zoom lens.

Different focal lengths are better suited to certain subjects, objects or styles, depending on what you're shooting.

35mm primes are good for 'street' photography, group portraits and some landscape shots because of the wide angle of view. 70-100mm primes make good 'portrait' lens with 85mm being the most popular. While a 50mm prime makes a good all round lens and is a good place to start.

It's also worth noting the depth of field provided by different focal length primes. A 100mm lens at f/2.8 will have much shallower depth of field than a 35mm at f/2.8 while framing the same shot. This helps when trying to blur the background or isolate the subject.

Also remember that these focal lengths are calibrated to full frame cameras. So if you are using a crop sensor, you'll need to multiply the focal length by 1.6x or 1.5x depending on the make of your camera.

Zoom/Telephoto Lens

With a zoom lens, the focal length can be varied. This allows you to zoom in and out to frame your subject without having to physically move closer or further away. A zoom lens might look something like this with various lenses inside:

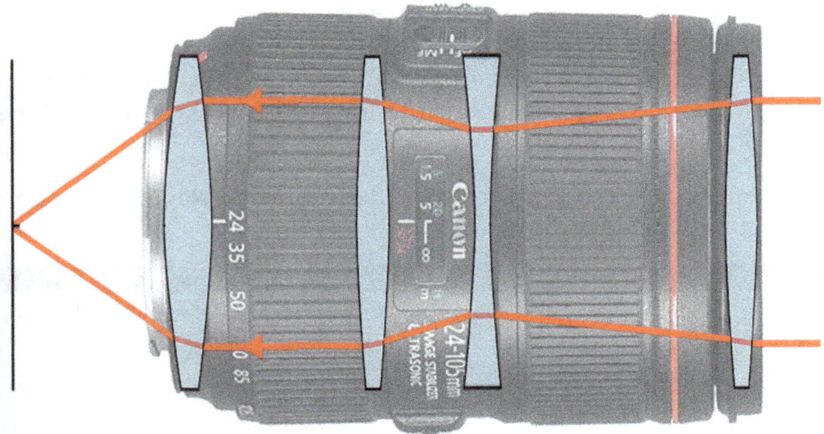

As you increase the focal length, the more you zoom in.

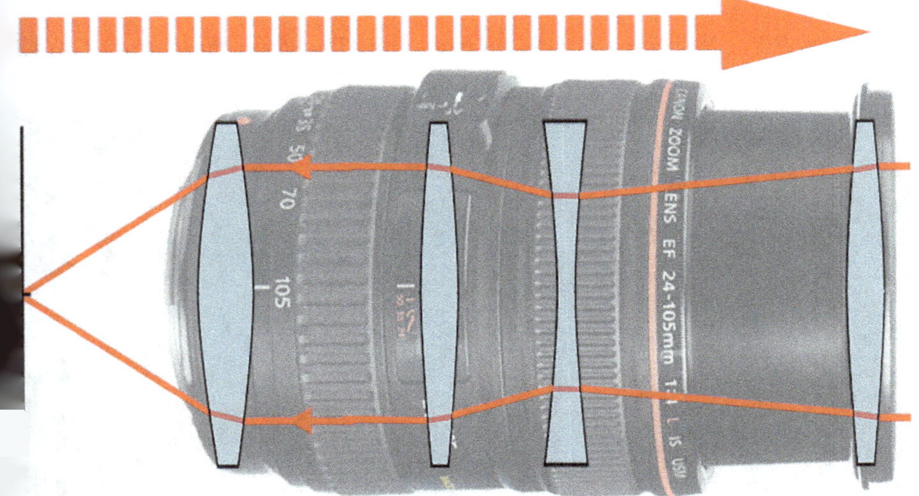

Zoom lenses provide greater versatility as you can change the focal length. This makes them ideal for sports photography, wildlife, or events where it isn't possible to get physically close to the subject.

There are an endless number of zoom lenses available, from 24-70mm up to 600mm and longer in some instances.

Chapter 3: Lenses

Zoom lenses have either a fixed aperture or a variable aperture. With fixed aperture zoom lenses, the aperture remains the same throughout the entire focal range, so if you set the aperture to f2.8 while zoomed out, it will remain at f2.8 when you zoom all the way in. Fixed aperture lenses are also larger, heavier, and more expensive.

Variable aperture zoom lenses are more affordable and lighter than their fixed aperture counterparts. The aperture varies throughout the focal range. So you might see a lens that has an aperture of f3.5 - f5.6. This means that when you are zoomed all the way out, the maximum aperture will be f3.5. As you zoom in, the aperture gradually stops down to f5.6.

There are generally three types of zoom lenses: wide angle, standard, and superzoom or telephoto.

Focal length		Use
18 - 70mm	Wide Angle	Architecture, Landscape, Street
70 - 200 mm	Standard Zoom	Portraiture and General
200 - 600+ mm	Superzoom/Telephoto	Sports and Wildlife

Remember that these focal lengths are calibrated to full frame cameras, if you are using a crop sensor, you need to multiply the focal length by 1.5x or 1.6x depending on the model of camera you're using.

Here is a 70 - 200mm fixed aperture lens. The aperture is set to f4.0 while zoomed out.

When you zoom in, the aperture remains the same.

All zoom lenses will have an optimal focal length where the focus is the sharpest, as well as an optimal aperture. This is known as the lens sweet spot. For most lenses, this is usually 2-4 f-stops down from the widest aperture. So on our 70-200mm lens, the widest aperture is 2.8, so you'd expect the sweet spot to be somewhere around f5.6 - f11.5 in normal lighting conditions. For low light environments, this rule isn't always possible to apply as you would need to stop down to f2.8 if there isn't enough light to expose the photo correctly.

This is a very rough guide and should be taken as such. The best thing to do is experiment and test your lens with your camera to see what settings produce the best results. Mount your camera on a tripod, focus on a subject and take a series of photos from the maximum aperture. Stop down 1 f-stop after each photo. Then compare them side by side and note which one is sharpest. Find a focus test chart.

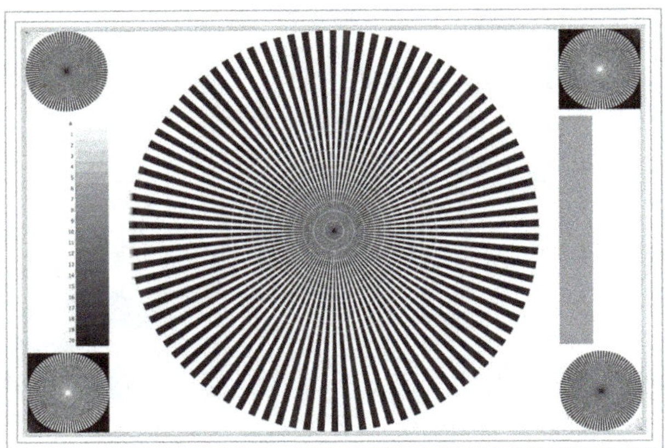

Macro Lens

A macro lens is a lens that specifically allows you to focus extremely close to a subject so that it appears large in the viewfinder.

Here is a photograph taken with a macro lens. This photo was taken using Canon EOS 7D camera, with a Canon 100mm f/2.8L macro lens (shown above).

I set the f-stops to f/4.0, and the shutter speed to 1/125sec with an ISO of 500.

Fisheye Lens

A fisheye lens is an ultra wide-angle lens that produces strong visual distortion intended to create a wide panoramic or hemispherical image.

Here is a photo taken with the fisheye lens pictured above.

You can see the wide angle shot and the distortion of the ground, trees and walls.

Lens Filters

Most camera filters screw onto the front of your lens, so you'll need to make sure you get the correct size filter for your particular lens.

Each lens filter delivers a specific effect. Filters are also great for protecting the front lens.

In this chapter, we'll take a look at some common filters

- Lens Filters

- UV filters

- Polarizing filters

- Neutral density filters

Filters are designed to restrict the light entering the lens. This helps to enhance colours, minimize lens glare and reflections from rivers, pools and windows.

There are various different types of filters such polarising filters, neutral density filters, UV filters and so on.

UV Filters

These are a bit redundant nowadays, since most modern lens optics deal with UV distortion quite well. A UV filter removes ultra-violet light rays that tend to make images look a bit hazy - especially shots taken in bright sunlight.

UV filters are also a great way of protecting the front of your lenses from smudges or scratches.

Polarizing Filters

If you remember from high-school physics, most light sources emit light in incoherent light waves ie light waves emitted at different angles. This is called unpolarised light.

Also light waves reflecting off shiny surfaces such as glass or water are polarised in a direction parallel to the surface.

Chapter 4: Lens Filters

Light rays entering the lens might look something like this. Notice that all the light rays are at different angles called planes. Some are at 90°, others at 45°, and so on.

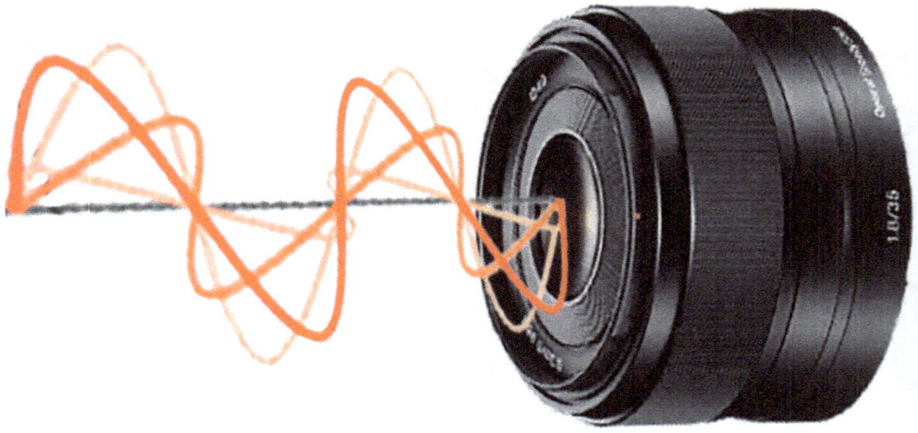

Polarisers restrict the light rays entering a lens and allows only light reflected from one plane, as shown below:

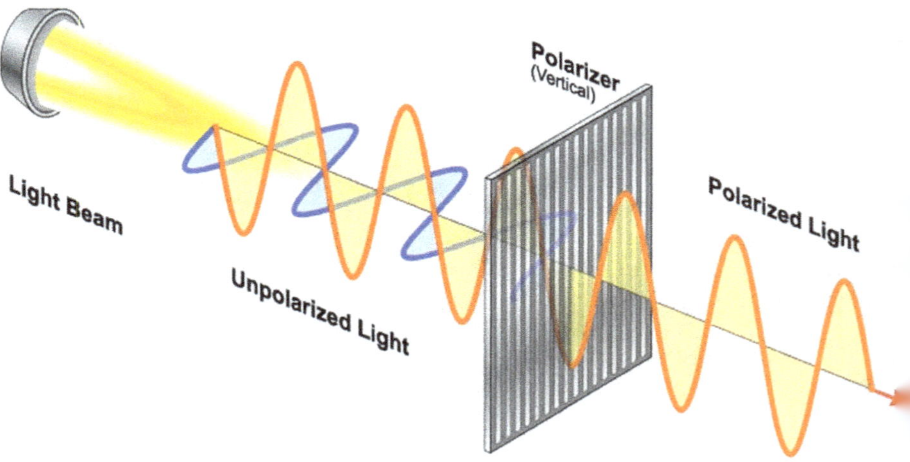

This can be used to saturate colours, darken skies or reduce reflection from glass or water.

Rotating the front of a polarizing filter regulates the effect, so they offe great flexibility.

Polarisers are a must-have for landscape photographers, and they b used to create stunning blue skies and beautiful clear shots of lake and rivers.

You can easily remove or at least reduce reflections with a polarising filter.

Reflections from lakes, rivers, or windows, as well as glare from bright skies can be reduced by rotating the filter to the correct angle. You'll need to look through the viewfinder and rotate the filter until you see the desired result.

Neutral Density Filters

Neutral density (ND) filters, work by reducing the amount of light entering the lens and come in a range of densities - the greater the density the less light is allowed to enter the lens. The left photo shown below has no filter attached - notice when trying to correctly expose the side of the mountain, the sky is blown out.

The image on the right has a 2 stop ND filter. Notice the sky shows up nicely, the shadows on the side of the mountain are richer and better exposed without blowing out the bright sky.

Graduated neutral density filters allow the photographer to balance the difference in brightness between the land and the sky.

Other Equipment

In this chapter, we'll take a look at some other equipment that is available.

We'll cover tripods for photography and ones designed for video.

We'll also cover bags and cases that you can buy to protect your camera and lenses.

- Photography Tripods

- Monopods

- Video Tripods

- Bags

Photography Tripods

Tripods come in various shapes and sizes. For still photography, you want a tripod that is lightweight and portable. One with an adjustable head allows you to line up and level your shot. Some tripods come with a spirit level bubble to help you to level your shot.

You'll also want a tripod with a quick release plate. This allows you to attach the plate to the bottom of the camera and slot it into place on top of the tripod. You can then remove the camera easily by releasing the plate.

A tripod with an adjustable height is a must.

Also make sure the tripod you're getting is strong enough to hold the weight of the camera. This is particularly important if you're using an SLR camera with a large lens.

Some tripods have other attachments you can use to position your camera in a variety of different orientations. With the tripod below, you can face your camera downwards, upwards, at an angle or to the side.

Monopods

A monopod allows you to hold your camera steady, allowing te you to take sharper pictures at slower shutter speeds, and/or with longer focal length lenses. Monopods are particularly useful for large heavy cameras and also taking photos in low light, at night, or for sports shots and wildlife photography.

Video Tripods

Video tripods are a little different. They have a fluid head that is designed to smooth out motion such as panning or tilting shooting.

Video tripods can be easier to line up and level your shot but are limited to pan or tilt, and don't have a feature for flipping the camera into portrait orientation.

Bags

You can get various different types of bags for your camera. The bag or case you get will greatly depend on what kit you have.

You can get bags that will hold your camera and a couple of lenses

Or you can get larger rug sacks with various compartments for the camera itself and lenses

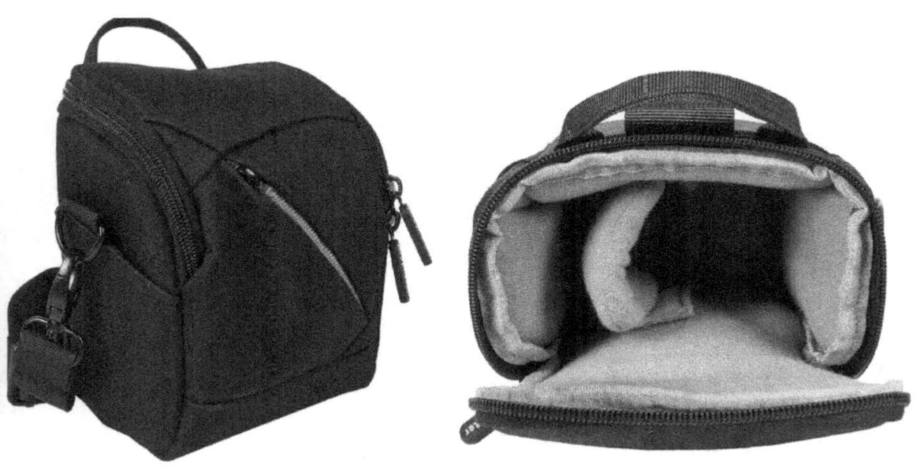

Smaller bags are also available for smaller cameras, or if you don't have a kit with lots of lenses

Lighting

Lighting plays an important role in photography, without it you wouldn't be able to take any photographs.

In any photograph, the light falls on the subject in a certain way, creating bright areas and dark areas. These highlights and shadows create contrast, which can make the photo more interesting but can also create problems in some situations.

Generally, the more light you have, the better your photos will turn out. However, you'll also need to think about the quality of the light, as some types of light are hard and some more flattering than others.

In this chapter, we'll take a look at

- Light Sources

- Light Modifiers

- Reflectors

- Hard, Soft, and Ambient lighting

Light Sources

Transmitted light is light that you can see emitted from a light source such as the sun, or artificial light. Reflected light is as its name suggests, light reflected off a surface or your subject.

For indoor photography, your light sources can include lamps, ceiling lights, sunlight through a window, and your camera's flash. This gives you more flexibility, as you can move lights or turn them on or off to control the direction and brightness of the lighting.

With continuous lighting, the lights remain on all the time and are good for beginners as what you see is what you get. This makes it easier to adjust lighting if necessary.

Speedlights are external flash units that produce an immense amount of light in an instant. They can also be mounted to the hot shoe on the top of the camera.

Strobe Lights are self-contained flash units with a power supply and a remote trigger. These are usually mounted on a stand and placed in position to light the subject when the photographer takes the photo.

Light Modifiers

The lights mentioned above create very harsh shadows and are very bright. In order to create various lighting effects, create mood or make the light more flattering, modifiers can be added in front of the light.

The first type is a diffuser. This softens the light and reduces the harsh shadows created by the naked lights. Diffusers can either be an umbrella that goes in-front of the light.

Or you can get a softbox. A softbox contains a light source inside the box with a white diffuser over the front.

You can use these with a strobe light or continuous light.

Reflectors

Reflectors are great for fixing odd shadows or even adding some colour to the subject. Here, the reflector is being used to fill in some shadows on the subject to help balance out the light.

There are different colours of reflector. Each colour has a different effect on the subject. White or silver is most common, but you can add differences with black or gold, as you can see below.

Silver   Gold   White   Black

Silver reflectors reflects the most light and are ideal for portraits. Gold reflectors produce a yellow/goldish hue. White is the most flexible and works both indoors and outdoors, its usually the best option and offers a more flattering light. A black reflector isn't really a reflector and actually absorbs light. It is good for when you have too much light in an area or part of the shot is over exposed.

Types of Light

When it comes to taking a good photo, the type of lighting that you use is one of the most important elements. There are many different types of light, but we'll concentrate on the basic types in order to make it easier to understand.

Ambient light is the general light illuminating a scene and not created by lights added to the scene by the photographer. Sunlight and daylight are considered ambient lighting, but so can a moonlight, house lights, a window or a streetlight.

Soft light is often diffused, creating shadows with edges that are soft with less contrast than hard light. It is achieved by adding a diffuser to a light source. In the photograph below, you can see the soft shadows on the left side of the face, and on the t-short. This gives a much softer look to the photo.

Hard light is the opposite of soft light and creates harsh shadows with high contrast. This type of light creates a more dramatic tone to photos, but can also be unflattering if used incorrectly. It is often achieved by using bright focused light sources. In the photo below, you can see the harsh shadows across the subject's face, as well as on the clothing. This gives a more dramatic feel to the photo

Lighting Angles

When lighting an object, you can place lights at different angles to create various effects.

Front Lighting

Placing the subject so that light is directly in front of the person or object, brings out the detail as there aren't any shadows in the image. However front lighting alone often looks very flat.

Side Lighting

Placing the light source at a 45° or 90° angle from the subject creates shadows, depth and mood. When doing this, watch where the shadows fall on the subject. Minor adjustments in the subject's position or the position of the light can create more effective shadows.

Back Lighting

Back lighting often serves to separate the subject from the background and makes them pop off the photograph. As you can see below, it creates a halo effect around the subject.

Background Lighting

This is when you have a lot of light in the background of your image. For example, placing the subject directly in front of a window.

To counter this effect, you could fire the flash. This is known as a fill flash.

7 Composing your Shot

Understanding the principles of composition in photography and knowing how to lead your viewer's eye to your subject or whatever focal point you want to them to look at.

In this chapter, we'll take a look at some common techniques to compose better photos

- Composing your Shot
- Lining up your Shots
- Rule of Thirds & Golden Ratio
- Golden Triangle
- Horizon Lines
- Vanishing Points
- Looking Room
- Head Room
- High Angle
- Low Angle
- Bird's Eye View
- Dutch Tilt
- Depth of Field

Take a look at the video resources. Open your web browser and navigate to the following site, or scan the code.

elluminetpress.com/composition

Lining up your Shots

There are a couple of well known techniques to help you line up your shots. First we'll take a look at the infamous rule of thirds which will help you to line up your shots. Then we'll take a look at the golden ratio which is a far better composition tool to use.

Rule of Thirds & Golden Ratio

When you're taking a photo, you can often make a photo look more natural by placing your subject off centre. This technique called the rule of thirds, and divides your photograph into sections that look a bit like a tic-tac-toe grid.

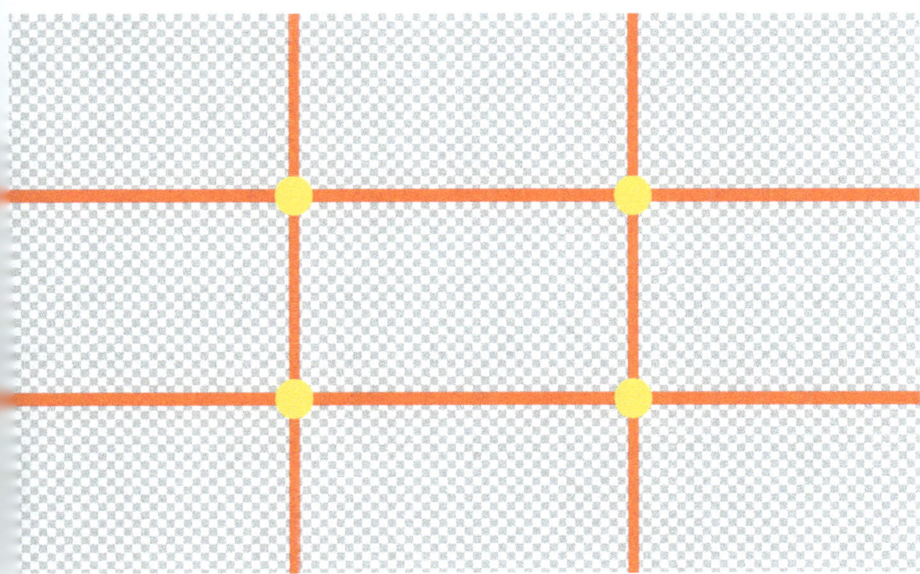

Where the lines cross is where you want to place your subject or object of interest. These are called power points.

I don't think the rule of thirds is a very good way to compose your shots, however it is usually the place everyone starts.

A much better approach is to use the golden ratio.

This divine ratio was used in architecture design, Leonardo Davinci used it in many of his paintings, and it appears in many forms in nature such as arrangements of leaves on plants, shells and human body proportions.

Chapter 7: Composing your Shot

This is not a maths lesson, so I'll spare you the theory behind the construction of the spiral. If you want to know more, go look up the Fibonacci sequence and golden spiral. When constructed, the spiral looks like this.

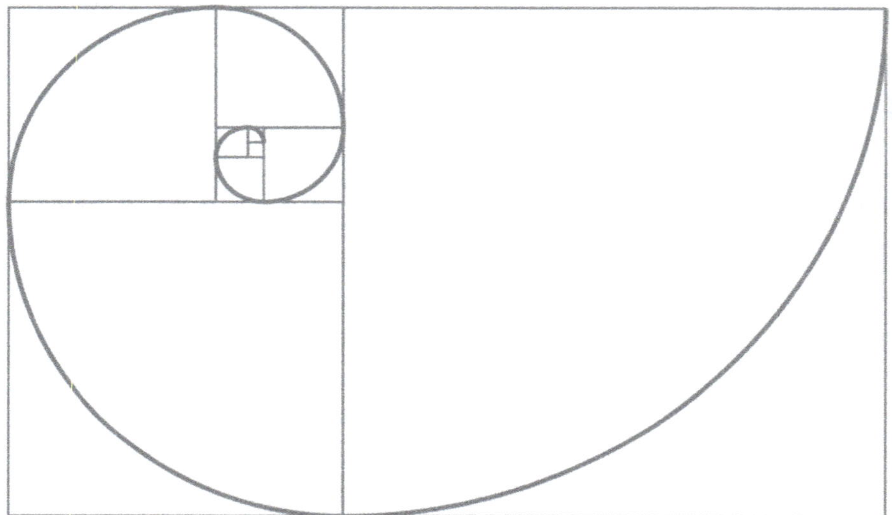

Depending on how you want to compose your photograph, you could flip the spiral and put it on top of another, as shown below. So you have two points of interest. One top left and one bottom right. The points of interest should be placed near the start of the spiral.

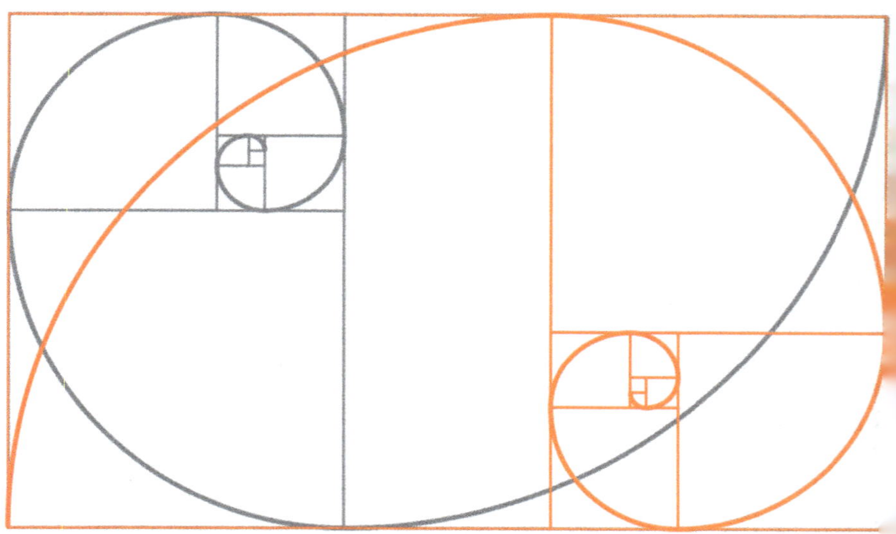

Similarly, you could rotate it again and fill in the top right and bottom left. When you do this, you'll notice something similar to the rule of thirds grid. This is called a Phi Grid.

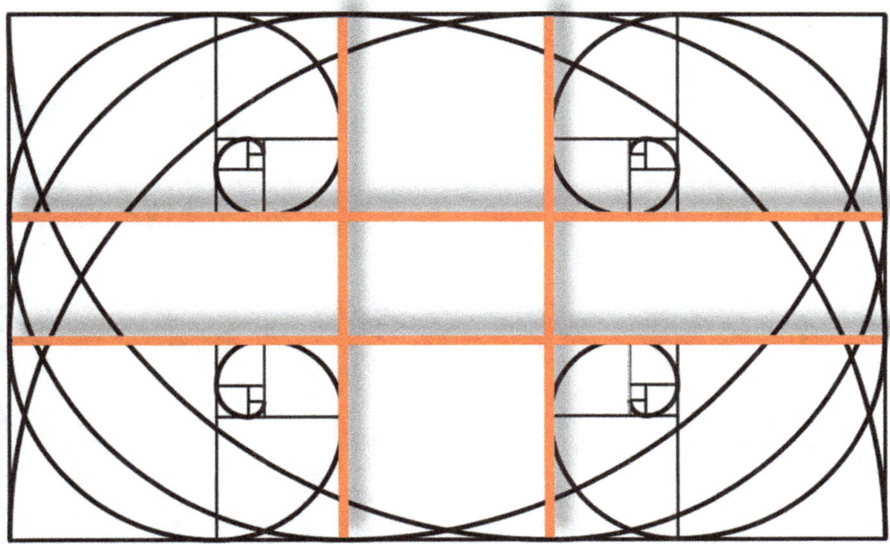

Use this grid in the same way as the rule of thirds grid. Line up the points of interest, in this case the bottle against the points where the grid lines cross. These are called the power points.

To use the golden spiral, place the small part over the point of interest. You can flip the spiral anyway around on the photograph. On close-ups such as he photo below, the point of interest is usually the face or more precisely the eyes. Here we've placed the spiral starting on the model's eye, with plenty of 'looking room' to the left.

Lets have a look at a landscape. The point of interest is the guy walking along the path, so we superimpose the golden spiral with the small part of the spiral over the guy in the photo.

Golden Triangle

The cross points on the triangle are in a similar position to the golden spiral we looked at earlier. The only difference is, with this composition method, you're looking for lines in your photograph.

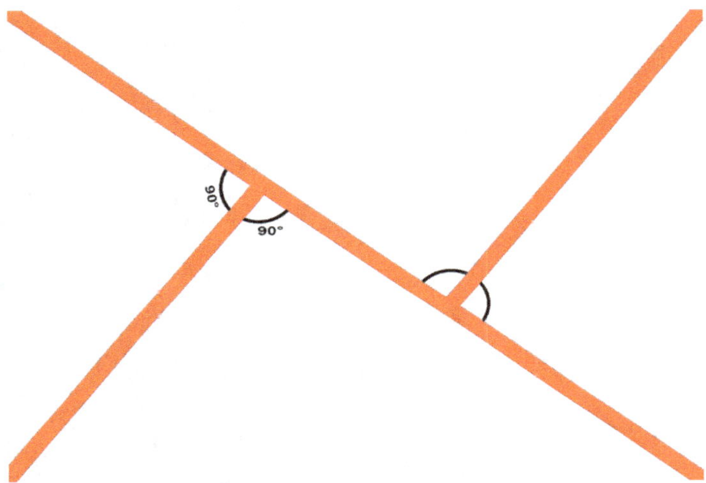

Lets have a look at an example. Here we can see the bridge forms a few lines going off into the distance. We can align the most prominent line with the dividing line on the golden triangle.

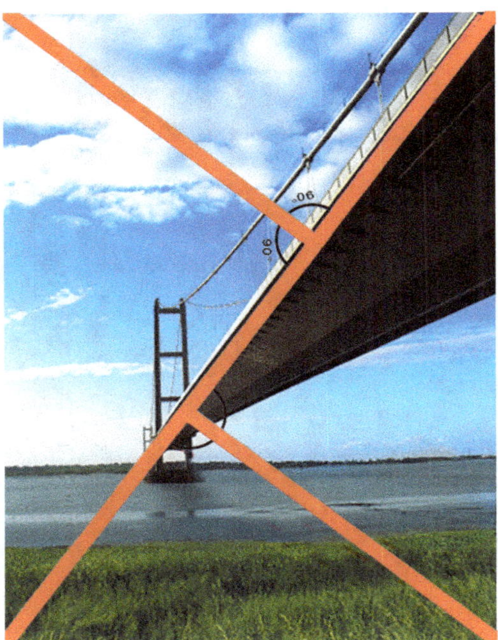

Chapter 7: Composing your Shot

Horizon Lines

Your horizon should be parallel to the horizontal lines, usually the bottom line on skyline photographs.

When taking photos of landscapes try and find a line such as a mountain range or coast line, this will give you something to focus on and line up your shot while keeping parallel to the horizon.

You could use the golden triangle method for this one.

Leading Lines

It makes a more interesting image when it naturally draw the eye along subtle, organic lines to a specific focal point. These can be vertical, horizontal, diagonal, converging, arcing, and so on.

Here, in the image below, your eye is lead along the train tracks into the distance, where you see the main subject of the photograph: the people walking. Notice the subject is positioned just off center using the golden ratio

In this photo below, you can see the leading lines, leading you into the distance, giving you the impression you're going around the corner.

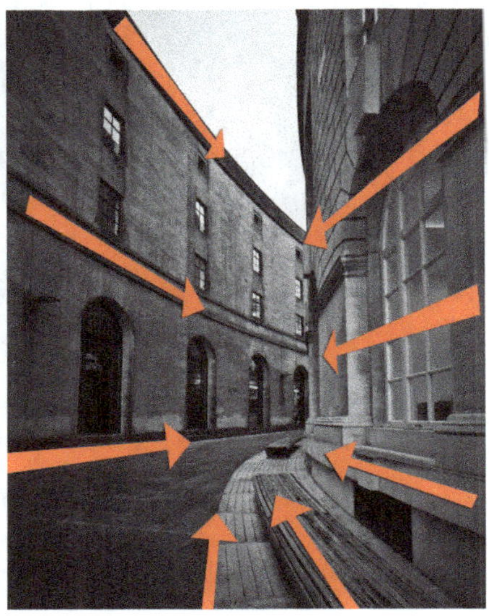

Vanishing Points

When taking photos along sides of buildings, look also for lines in the building structure, this will help you line up your shot as all these lines (highlighted below in red) will converge into what is known as the vanishing point. This gives a sense of depth to your photo

Also keep any vertical lines in the structures parallel to the vertical lines on the 3rds grid as highlighted in yellow. This will keep your shot level.

Another good tip is to keep your camera at the same level as your subject for a more neutral photograph.

Looking Room

With close up shots of people, include some looking room if they're not looking at the camera. Include some of the background to give a bit of depth and interest.

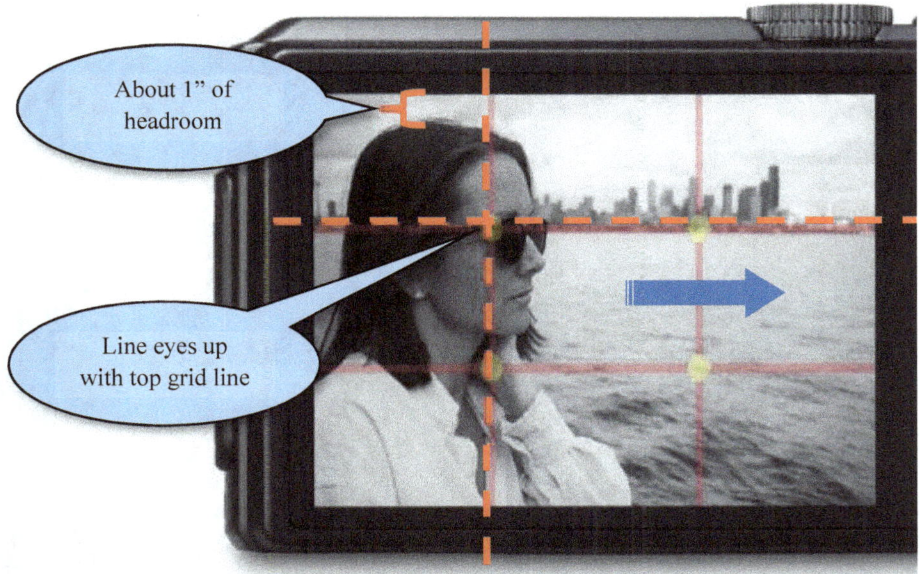

The subject doesn't always have to look at the camera, and if they're not, then subject should always be 'looking into the frame' and not have their nose pressed against the side of the photograph.

Head Room

For closeup and head shots, try getting the subjects face by the power points on the golden ratio grid or rule of thirds grid. Photos like this are usually used as profile pictures or even passport/driver's license photos.

Aim to get about 1" of head room between the subject's head and the top of the frame. You can also include a couple of inches of their shoulders. Make sure the background is clear.

Shoot at a slight angle rather than face on. Rotate the subject's body slightly way from the camera (about 10-30 degrees), then turn the subject's head back to make eye contact with the camera. Subtle, but it will give your headshot a more professional feel.

Make sure you set the focus point on the eyes and don't use a harsh flash. Either add a flash diffuser or use a soft light source. a bright flash is very unflattering.

For a mid waist shot, leave about 1" of headroom above the subject's head.

Similarly at the bottom of your frame, leave about an inch or two under the elbows.

Depth

Try adding some depth to your photographs. Getting a close-up object on one of the lower power points can add some depth to a photograph with the houses in the mid ground and the mountain range in the background.

You could have someone sitting on the bench close up with the houses around in the mid ground and the mountain range in the background.

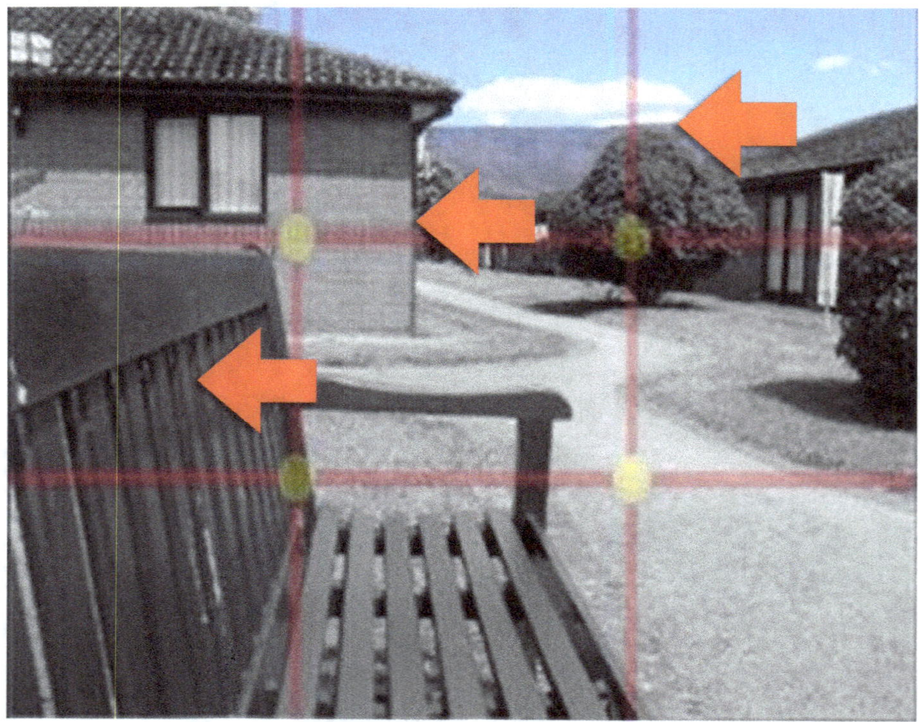

You can experiment with different apertures, to focus on the foreground and slightly blur the background, or you could have the whole thing in focus.

You could also turn it around. Focus in the distance, with an object in the foreground out of focus.

You want to take the viewer on a journey so to speak and guide the viewer's eye around the image. You can do this with the focus, the object in focus will automatically guide the viewer's eye to that object.

Try experimenting with different arrangements with some objects in focus and out of focus.

In the photo of the river below, get some water movement by the rocks in the foreground and the rest of the river and some trees in the background.

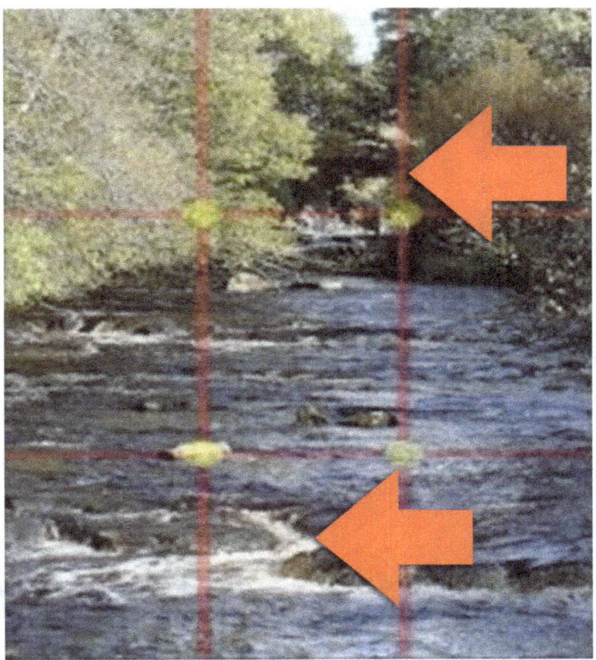

Try to use the surroundings to your advantage rather than just have your subject in the centre of the frame all the time.

You could focus on an object in the foreground, perhaps a branch, and leave the background out of focus.

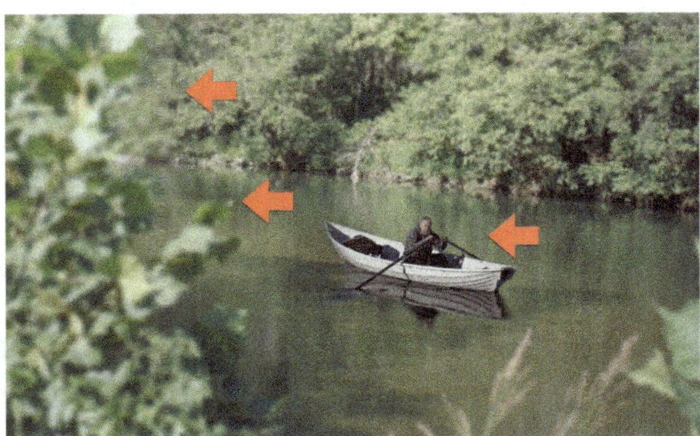

Or you could flip it around and focus on something in the distance, with over hanging branches or trees out of focus in the foreground.

High Angle

A high angle shows the subject from above, i.e. the camera is angled down towards the subject. This has the effect of diminishing the subject, making them appear less powerful, less significant or even submissive. For high angle shots, get yourself a good monopod.

Don't always shoot your photographs from natural head height. Try high angles and low angles. Just make sure you keep your camera horizontally level.

Low Angle

Low angle shows the subject from below, giving them the impression of being more powerful or dominant.

So experiment, don't always shoot things from eye level, depending on what you're covering, changing the height of the camera relative to the subject can have a dramatic effect on how they're perceived on screen.

Bird's Eye

The scene is shown from directly above. This is a completely different and somewhat unnatural point of view which can be used for dramatic effect or for showing a different spatial perspective and scale. You can achieve shots like the one below using a monopod or crane.

For aerial and really hight shots, you'll need to use a drone.

Or find a high vantage point to shoot from.

Dutch Tilt

This method pretty much breaks all the rules and is achieved by slightly tilting the camera either to the left or right. Notice the horizon line marked in red below.

This can be used for dramatic effect to portray unease, tension, disorientation, frantic or desperate action, intoxication, madness, etc.

Depth of Field

The depth of field (DOF) is the distance between the nearest and farthest objects in a scene that appear in focus.

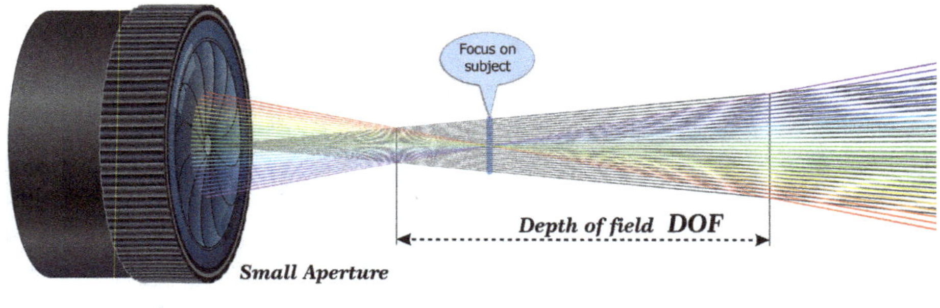

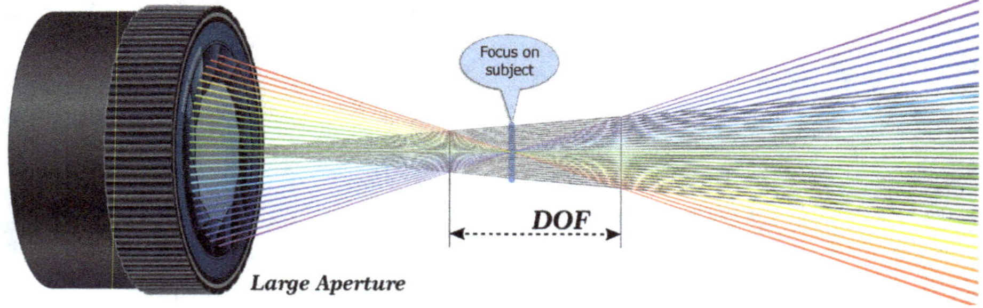

Large apertures produce a shallow depth of field, so is really useful if you want to take a photo of something and throw the background out of focus.

You can use the depth of field to great effect. For example, you can lock your focus on an object and blur the background, thereby shifting the viewer's attention.

The photo below was taken using a 85mm lens with an aperture set to f1.2, shutter speed set to 1/325 with an ISO of 100. The high shutter speed freezes the action clearly. This blur effect in the background is known as bokeh.

Here's another example of depth of field in the photo below. You can see the flowers in focus in the middle, with the foreground and background out of focus. This give the photo some depth.

Exposing your Shot

Iris or aperture setting, shutter speed and ISO setting.

In this chapter, we'll explore the aperture, shutter speed and ISO settings.

- Aperture

- Shutter Speed

- ISO

- Exposure Triangle

- White Balance

- Metering Modes

- Focus Modes

Take a look at the video resources. Open your web browser and navigate to the following website, or scan the code.

elluminetpress.com/camset

Aperture

Sometimes called an iris, the aperture controls the amount of light reaching the image sensor in the camera, and also has an effect on the depth of field.

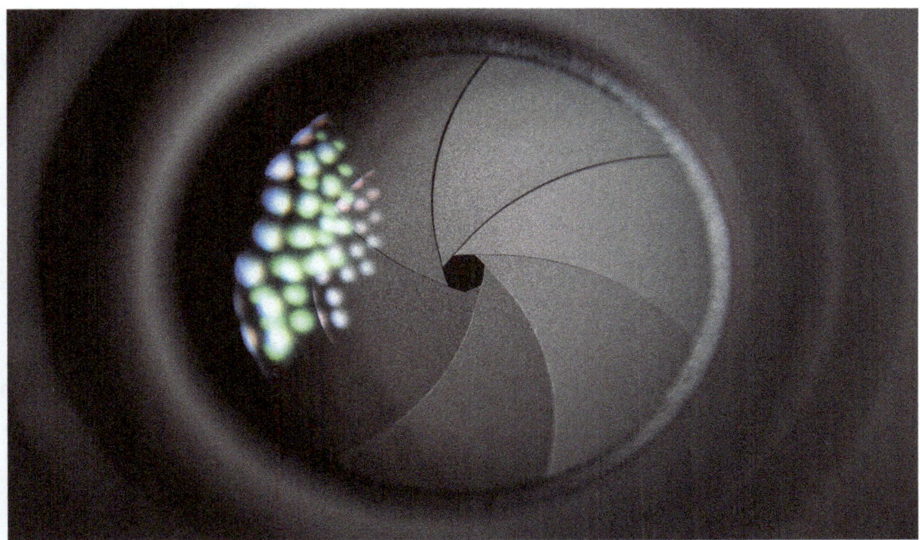

The aperture is measured in f-stops and is defined as the ratio of the focal length of the lens to the diameter of the aperture. The lower the number the wider the aperture.

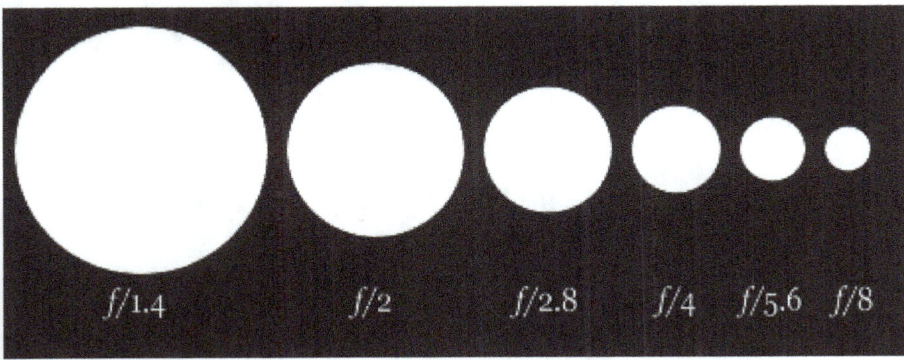

You might have also heard the term 'lens speed' or 'fast lens'. This has nothing to do with shutter speed. Lens speed refers to the maximum aperture the lens is capable of. Fast lenses have an aperture around f1.2, f1.4, f1.8, or f2.8. These lenses are ideal for low light environments.

Remember, the lower the f/number the wider the aperture.

Shutter

The shutter speed is the length of time the camera's image sensor is exposed to the scene you're photographing, and is measured in fractions of a second.

Shutter speeds available to you on your camera will usually double with each setting:

1/500, 1/250, 1/125, 1/60, 1/30, 1/15, 1/8

This 'doubling' is handy to keep in mind as aperture settings also double the amount of light that is let in – as a result increasing shutter speed by one stop and decreasing aperture by one stop should give you similar exposure levels.

Using a slow shutter speed of 1 second.

Using a fast shutter speed of 1/250 second.

How you adjust the shutter speed depends on what you're trying to achieve.

Generally if you want to freeze a fast moving object, you choose a faster shutter speed. If you want to blur motion, you choose a slower shutter speed.

Here's a rough guide.

	Shutter Speed
Stars	30"
Blur moving water	1" - 5"
Fast moving people	1/250
Landscapes	1/125
Sports	1/125 and over
Wildlife	1/150 and over
Airshow	1/150 to 1/1000
Birds in flight	1/1000 and over
Sports	1/500 to 1/1000

Don't let these rules inhibit your creativity. Experiment with different shutter speeds and see what happens.

To freeze the action on this shot, the photographer used a 250mm zoom lens with a shutter speed of 1/800, and an aperture of f4. The ISO was set quite low to 400.

ISO

In traditional photography where rolls of film were used, the ISO was the indication of how sensitive the film was to light. It was measured in ISO numbers such as ISO100, ISO200, and ISO400 etc. The lower the ISO number the lower the sensitivity of the film and the finer the grain in the photographs.

With digital photography, the ISO number indicates the sensitivity of the image sensor. This can be adjusted in the camera settings and the same principles apply as in film photography - the lower the number, the less sensitive your camera is to light, and the finer the grain of the photograph.

Higher ISO settings are can be used in darker situations to get faster shutter speeds. For example, if you are shooting an indoor sports event when you want to freeze the action in lower light, or taking photos of your favourite band in concert.

The image below was taken with an ISO setting of 128,000. Notice how grainy the image is.

Higher ISO settings tend to produce shots with more grain as can be seen here with the ISO setting on high.

For best results, you want to try to keep the ISO as low as possible.

Exposure Triangle

The Exposure Triangle is the term that is used to explain how aperture, shutter speed, and ISO all work together. These three parameters govern the amount of light that reaches sensor and how sensitive the sensor is to the light.

For example, the depth of field is controlled by the aperture. At the same time, the shutter speed can blur or freeze the action, and the ISO can compensate for lighting levels.

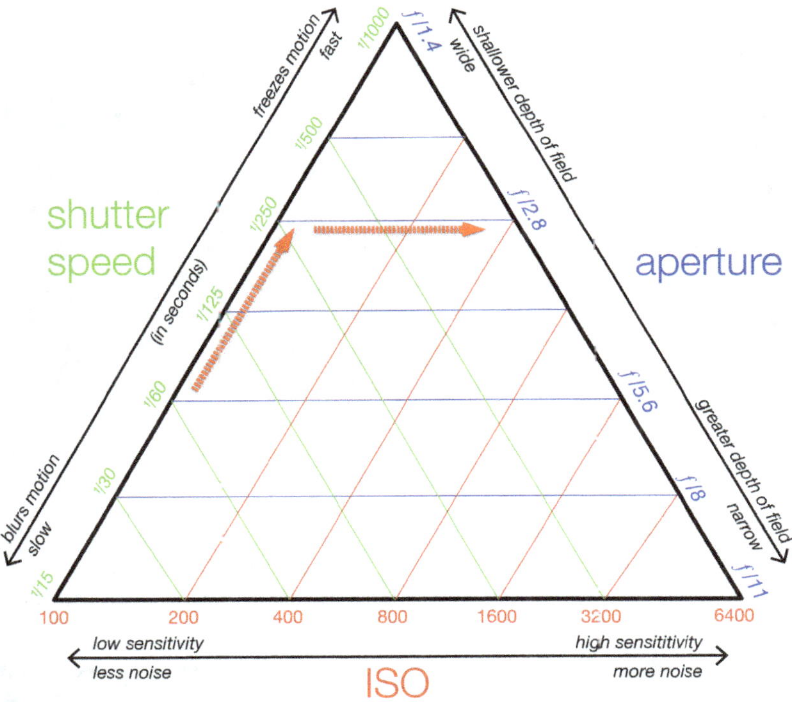

As you can see in the diagram above, the more you increase the shutter speed, the less light will hit your camera's sensor. This is great for freezing fast moving objects, but will make the image darker.

In order to compensate, you'll need to open the aperture. Opening the aperture will decrease the depth of field, meaning background objects will be out of focus. If you want the background in focus, you'll need to increase the ISO instead of the aperture. Keep in mind that increasing the ISO will add more digital noise to your image.

It's all about having the right balance of all three parameters to create good exposure.

Chapter 8: Exposing your Shot

Let's take a look at an example. I want to take a photograph in the daylight and I want to throw the background out of focus.

First, because we're shooting in broad daylight, so I can set the ISO quite low to 100 or 200.

Second, I want to blur the background. To do this, I need to open the aperture. This will reduce the depth of field, but will also allow far too much light into the camera and over expose the image.

To compensate for this, I need to increase the shutter speed. A high shutter speed will also freeze the action nicely and create a clear image.

For the shot above, I used a 300 mm zoom lens, set the aperture to f/4.0, the shutter speed to 1/500, and the ISO to 100

If on the other hand, I want include more of the background - ie the leaves on the right in the photo below, I need to close the aperture a bit to increase the depth of field, and decrease the shutter speed to compensate for less light entering the camera.

For this shot I used a 300mm zoom lens, set the aperture to f/6, the shutter speed to 1/250, and the ISO to 100

White Balance

Think of a reddish-yellow sky at sunset, while at noon the sky appears mostly blue. You need to compensate for the differences in the light. Most of the time the camera does a good job at measuring this, however it can improve your photographs especially those shot under artificial light - fluorescent lights, tungsten lights, and other household lights. This control this with the white balance setting on your camera.

Light sources appear to have slightly different colours, some are bright white, some are a bit more orangey, some have a yellow tint. This can give your photo either a reddish look (warm colour temperature) or a bluish look (cooler colour temperature).

Because of this, the white balance on the camera is there to control how the colour temperature of the light source you are shooting under will be recorded, either "cooler" (blue tint) or "warmer" (red tint).

For a normal photograph you want to get the colour as neutral as possible without any blue or red tint, unless you are using it to artistic effect.

Below is a table of light sources and the relative pre-set settings on the camera.

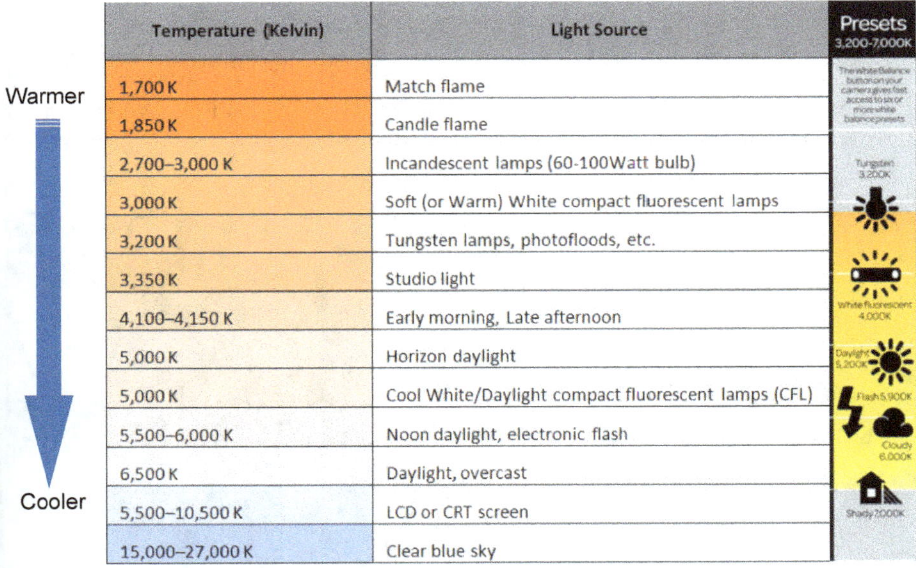

	Temperature (Kelvin)	Light Source	Presets 3,200–7,000K
Warmer	1,700 K	Match flame	The white balance button on your camera gives fast access to six or more white balance presets
	1,850 K	Candle flame	
	2,700–3,000 K	Incandescent lamps (60-100Watt bulb)	Tungsten 3,200K
	3,000 K	Soft (or Warm) White compact fluorescent lamps	
	3,200 K	Tungsten lamps, photofloods, etc.	
	3,350 K	Studio light	
	4,100–4,150 K	Early morning, Late afternoon	White fluorescent 4,000K
	5,000 K	Horizon daylight	Daylight 5,200K
	5,000 K	Cool White/Daylight compact fluorescent lamps (CFL)	Flash 5,900K
	5,500–6,000 K	Noon daylight, electronic flash	Cloudy 6,000K
	6,500 K	Daylight, overcast	
Cooler	5,500–10,500 K	LCD or CRT screen	Shady 7,000K
	15,000–27,000 K	Clear blue sky	

Look on the side of the bulb and you'll see a kelvin rating, usually indicated with a capital K. Set your camera's white balance to the same number.

Metering

Metering assesses the amount of light available in a particular scene, and calculates exposure settings on the camera accordingly. *Note that the metering meters from the centre of the frame not the focus point.*

Spot Metering is helpful for photographing back-lit subjects. The metering is calculated according to the very centre of the shot – a very small area of the frame.

Centre Weighted Metering means the camera will take information from numerous points around the frame but will give more emphasis to those in the centre. Like spot metering, this is good to use in tricky lighting situations where you don't need to identify very small parts of the image to meter on.

Focus Modes

Spot or 1 point focus, the camera focuses on a very precise area of the frame usually the centre.

Multiple Points such as 11, 23 or even 65 point Area Focus, will lock onto multiple focus points in your frame.

Manual focus gives full control of the lens allowing the photographer to adjust the focus accordingly.

Taking Pictures

In this chapter, we're going to take a look at taking photos using a DSLR or higher end camera, and put into practice what we learned in the previous chapters on lenses, composition and exposure.

This is where you can experiment with shutter speed, aperture, ISO, as well as the composition techniques we covered earlier.

Allow your creativity to flow and see what you come up with. As you practice, you'll rely less on all the rules and technical knowhow, and more on your eye.

We'll go through

- Shooting Modes

- Low Light Photography

- Night Photography

- Using a Flash

- Freezing the Action

Take a look at the video resources. Open your web browser and navigate to the following website, or scan the code.

elluminetpress.com/takepic

Shooting Modes

On most SLR and higher end cameras, you'll have a dial or control that
will allow you to put the camera into various shooting modes.

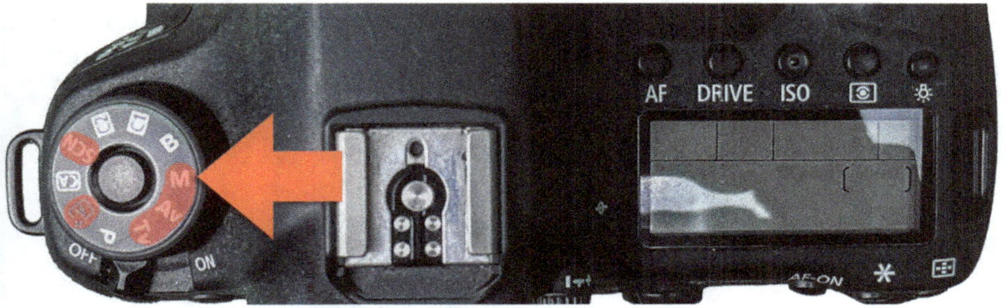

Auto Mode (A+)

Auto mode is useful for quick snapshots, but often produces undesirable
effects in low light and leaves no room for creativity with your photos.
Don't bother using it for any serious photography.

Aperture Priority (AV)

You set a specific aperture, and the camera automatically selects the
shutter speed. This is used when you want to control the depth of field.

Shutter Priority (TV)

You set a specific shutter speed and the camera automatically selects
the aperture. This is used when the subject you're shooting is moving
quickly and want to freeze the action.

Full Manual Control (M)

You set a specific shutter speed, aperture, and ISO. This is used when
you want complete control of the camera settings.

Preset Scenes (SCN)

These are factory presets that are calibrated to a specific scene, such
as a portrait, night shot, fast moving and so on. Useful for a quick
shot but often not very useful. Don't bother using them for any serious
photography.

Low Light Photography

Taking photos at night can be challenging, since your camera doesn't have a lot of light to work with.

Common problems such as blurry photos due to a slow shutter speed, grainy photos due to a high ISO number or dark photos if your camera can't compensate for the low light.

Try increasing the ISO setting, you can manually raise the ISO number in your camera's settings. This may reduce blurriness, but it may also make your photo grainier.

Increase the shutter speed.

Use a fast lens, and open the aperture as wide as you can.

	Flash	ISO	Aperture	Shutter Speed
Indoors/Party/Low light	Off	High	Wide	**Fast** to freeze action
City Lights	Off	Low	Med	**Slow** for movement effect – see bridge photo below
Stars	Off	Low	Med	**Slow**
Light Painting	Off	Low	Narrow	**Slow** - see bridge photo below
Fireworks	Off	Low	Med	**Slow** for movement effect – see fireworks photo

Turn the flash off on your camera.

You can also use the exposure compensation. If your photos are still coming out too dark, you can adjust the exposure compensation to increase the brightness. Although this will make the photos brighter, it won't actually improve the quality, so it's not really a substitute for more lighting.

Night Photography

Using slow shutter speeds to take photos can produce some spectacular effects.

This shot of the bridge was taken at night with the camera mounted on a tripod. To take this shot, I set the aperture to f/4 to let in enough light to capture the bridge itself and the headlights of the cars. I then used a shutter speed between 10-30 seconds - enough time to create the light trails. I also had to set the ISO as low as I could get it without underexposing the shot, as a high ISO is set in this situation would result in a lot of digital noise.

Fireworks can be tricky to shoot. For the shot below, I set the ISO to a low 200. To get everything in focus, I closed the aperture down to f/11. Depending on the lens you're using, you might need to open the aperture up a bit to about f/8.

I set up the camera on a tripod, and used a shutter speed of a couple of seconds, or use bulb mode if your camera has it. This made sure I captured the light streaks across the sky as the fireworks exploded. A fast shutter speed will freeze the action. The settings with greatly depend on the environment you're shooting in, so take a few test shots.

The lens I used was a Canon EF 70-200mm f/2.8L

Another tip when taking photos of fireworks, is to use manual focus, as the auto focus tends to have trouble focussing in the dark.

Using a Flash

If your camera has a built-in flash, then that can add a lot more light, but it can also be harsh and unflattering, although the flash is of little effect if the subjects are over 15 feet away. As you can see in the photo below, the harsh light from the flash completely washes out the facial features leaving ugly shadows around the eyes and nose.

If you need to use a flash, you can get external speedlight flashes that attach to the hot shoe on the top of your camera. With these flash units, you can add a diffuser to soften the light.

When using the flash, remember to lower your ISO to about 100.

You can also adjust the flash intensity on some units. This particular model goes from -3 to +3 in 1/3 stop increments.

Adjust your aperture and shutter speed (don't go higher than the flash sync speed). Tweak the ISO if necessary.

Set your shutter speed to the correct value. Check the Sync Speed on the flash unit, this is the speed at which the camera can use flash, usually 1/250. If you set a shutter speed faster then the sync speed, you'll start to get black banding across the photograph.

Freezing the Action

Photographing a fast-moving subject can be challenging. However the key to capturing any kind of fast motion is to use a fast shutter speed.

DSLRs and bridge cameras allow you to adjust the shutter speed manually using the Shutter Priority Mode, or Manual Mode to set a fast shutter speed. If you are using a point-and-shoot camera, you can select the Sports Scene Mode.

These shots can be particularly tricky if you are trying to take a photo of a fast moving sports game or a race.

In the image below, a bit of motion blur in the background can be used to great effect as long as the subject is in focus. This gives the impression that the car is moving very quickly.

This shot was taken with a slower shutter speed, while locking the focus on the car and panning across the scene to keep the car in the frame. The effect blurs the background giving the impression the car is moving fast. If I had chosen a faster shutter speed, this would have frozen the background and given the impression the car was standing still.

When taking fast moving sports shots, a good feature to use is burst mode, this allows continuous shooting of multiple shots every second as long as you are holding down the shutter button.

In the shot below, I used a 200mm lens, a shutter speed of 1/250, the aperture set to f8.0, with an ISO of 100.

'his was enough to freeze the action of the birds in flight.

10 Touching up Photos

For best results, it is always advisable to shoot your photographs in RAW format, rather than JPG. This allows a lot more flexibility when it comes to post production - adjusting brightness, shadows, contrast, colour and so on.

Think of RAW files along the same lines as a negative as was used in the old film days; or digital negative today. You process your RAW photos then save them out as JPG to use on the web, post on social media or some design project. This means you always have a copy of your original photograph you can go back to.

In this chapter, we'll take a look at getting your photos onto your computer and some basic photo editing techniques. We are going to use Adobe Lightroom Classic, Adobe Bridge and Photoshop, but you can also use free alternatives such as Microsoft Photos App with the RAW image extension, and Google Photos in Windows, or the Photos App on a Mac, and GIMP.

Check out the resources on the website

elluminetpress.com/photo

Import Photos

You can either import photos using Adobe Bridge or Lightroom. These are two separate Adobe applications and will not be covering these here, our focus is Photoshop.

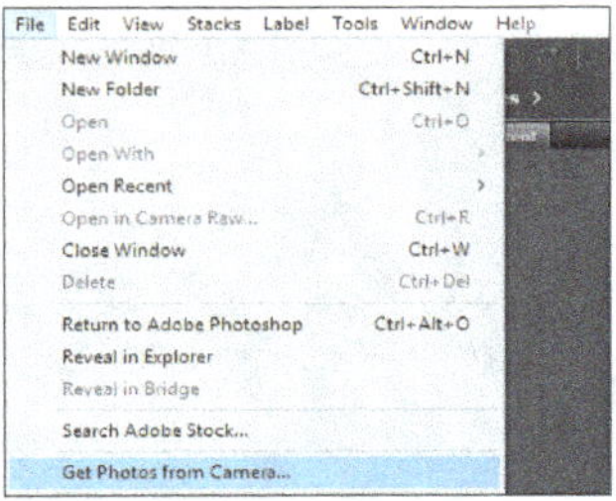

In Adobe Bridge, click the file menu and select 'get photos from camera'. From the dialog box that appears click 'advanced dialog' on the bottom left.

Click the tick box on the top left of each image you want to import. On the right hand side, select 'browse'.

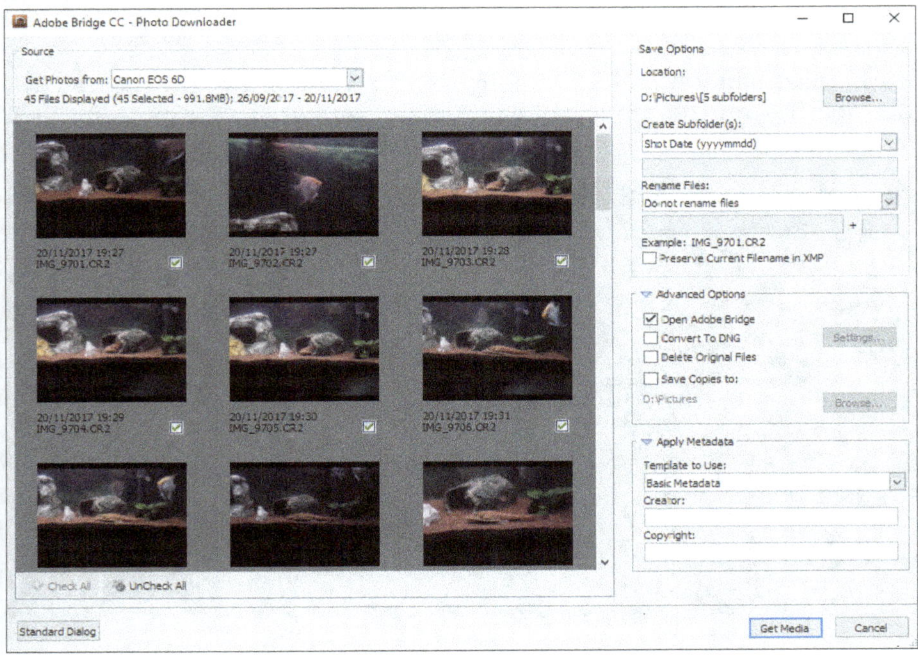

This is the folder on your computer where you want Bridge to store all your photos. I usually select the 'pictures' directory. Once you're done click 'Get Media' on the bottom right.

Chapter 10: Touching up Photos

If you have Lightroom, connect your camera and hit 'import' on the bottom left of the screen.

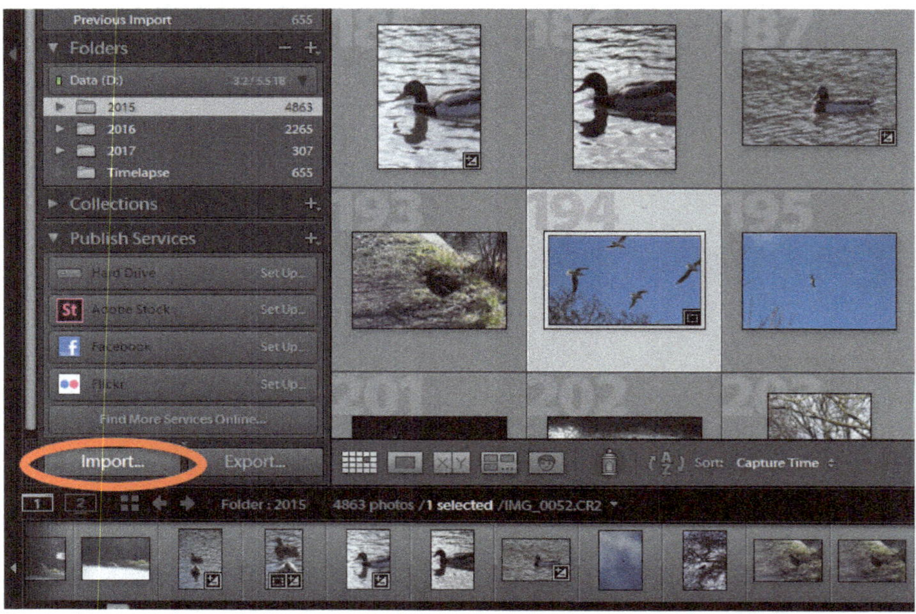

In the next window, select the photos you want to import. Either click the tick box on the top left of each image you want to import, or click 'import all' if you want to import every photo on your camera.

On the right hand side, select 'destination'. This is the folder on your computer where you want Lightroom to store all your photos. I usually select the 'pictures' directory. Once you're done click 'import' on the bottom right.

You can open any image in Photoshop from Lightroom. Right click on the image thumbnail, go down to 'edit in', then select 'Photoshop...'.

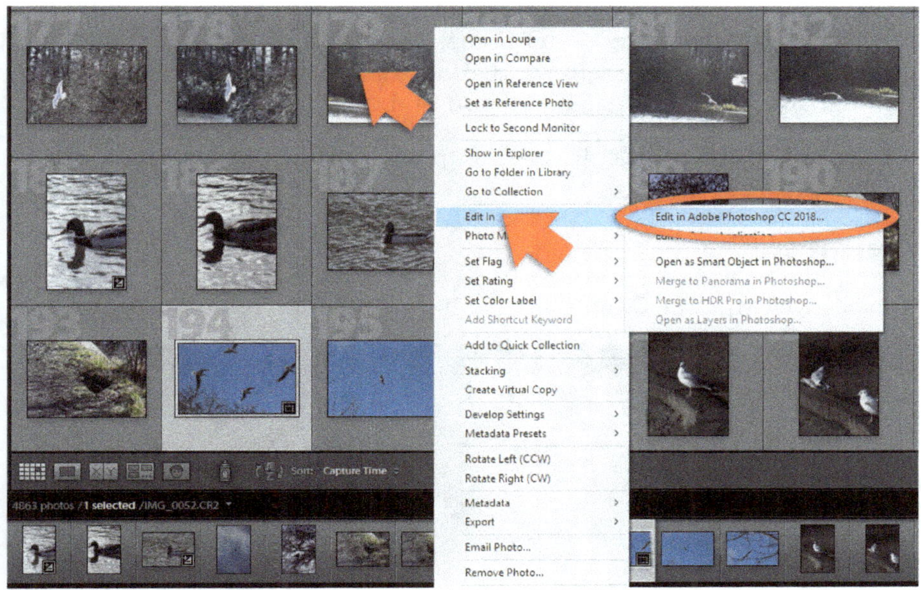

If you have adjusted the photograph in Lightroom you may be prompted with a few options. If not, the photo will open up in Photoshop.

If you want Lightroom to open the photo with the adjustments you have made, select 'edit a copy with Lightroom adjustments'. In not select 'edit original'.

Camera RAW

Camera RAW is your digital darkroom where you can adjust a photograph's exposure, brightness, adjust highlights or shadows, correct white balance, remove digital noise, as well as straighten up photographs, remove lens distortion and crop bits out.

Camera RAW automatically opens up when you open up a RAW image taken with your camera.

Opening

You can also find the Camera RAW filter on the filter menu in Photoshop.

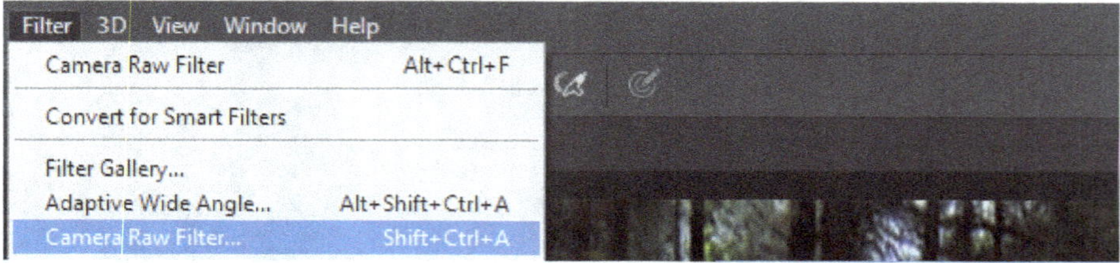

Lets take a look at the Camera RAW window.

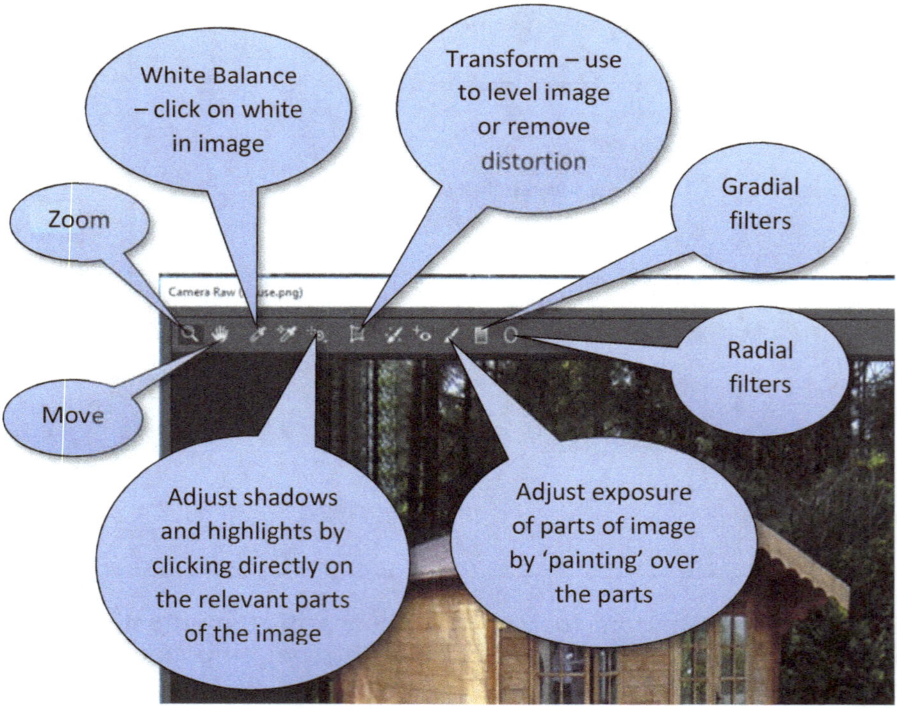

Reading a Histogram

The histogram shows the tonal range of a photograph - the range of brightness levels from pure black to pure white in the photo.

If all your peaks are squashed over to the left, the photograph is under exposed or too dark.

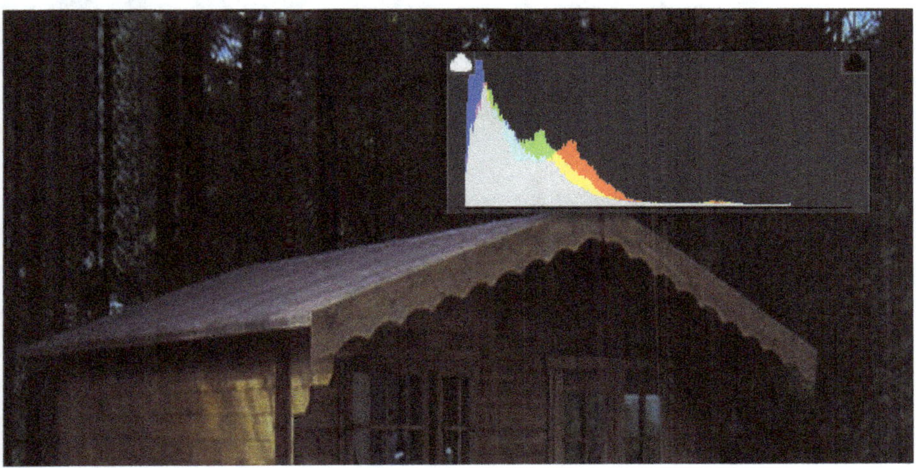

If all the peaks are squashed over to the right, your photo is over exposed or too bright.

This isn't always the case and depends on the photograph. For example, if a photograph has a lot of dark areas and shadows, then the histogram peaks will be more over to the left.

Chapter 10: Touching up Photos

Lets take a closer look at the histogram. The histogram is split into five sections: Blacks, Shadows, Midtones, Highlights & Whites.

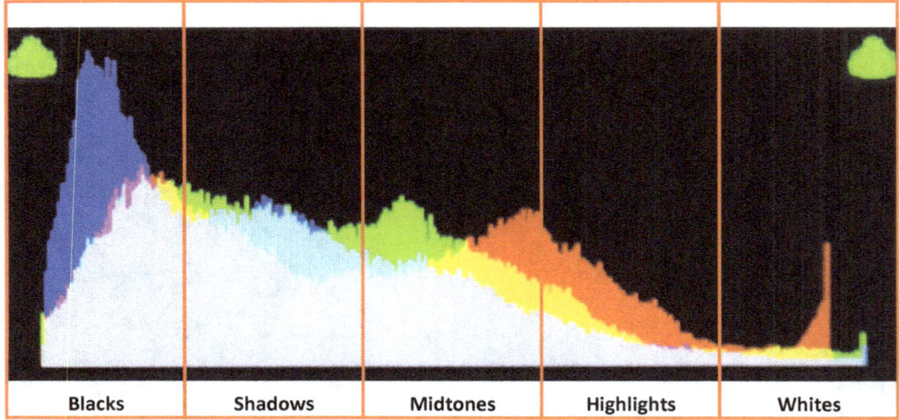

On a good histogram, most tones fall in the middle portion of the graph (shadows, midtones and highlights) with little or nothing at the extreme edges.

Also on the histogram you'll notice some colour. Photoshop histograms show the brightness levels for all the primary colours: red, green & blue channels (it also shows primary colours for print: yellow, cyan & magenta).

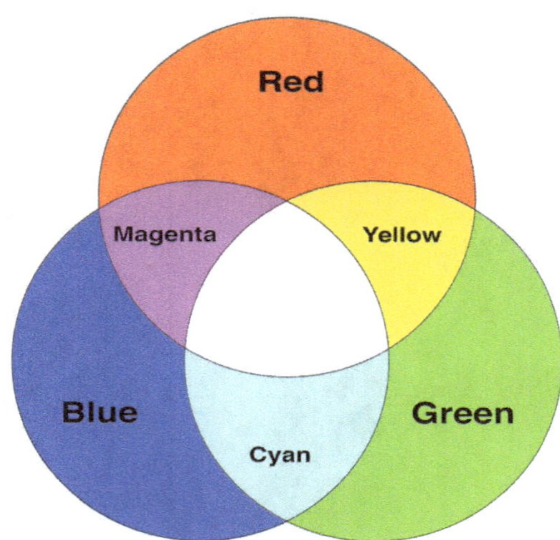

The light grey peak is the overall brightness. Don't worry too much about this now, for the scope of this exercise, concentrate on getting the peaks distributed across the five sections to achieve good exposure

Adjusting a Photo

Open up **cameraraw.cr2** and have a go at adjusting the blacks, shadows, midtones, highlights and whites using the camera raw filter, until you get a nice evenly spread histogram. Keep an eye on the photograph to make sure looks evenly exposed. This photo was shot with a canon camera in raw format.

To adjust the photo, use the highlights, shadows, whites and blacks sliders to adjust the relevant levels on the histogram. Use the exposure slider to adjust the overall brightness.

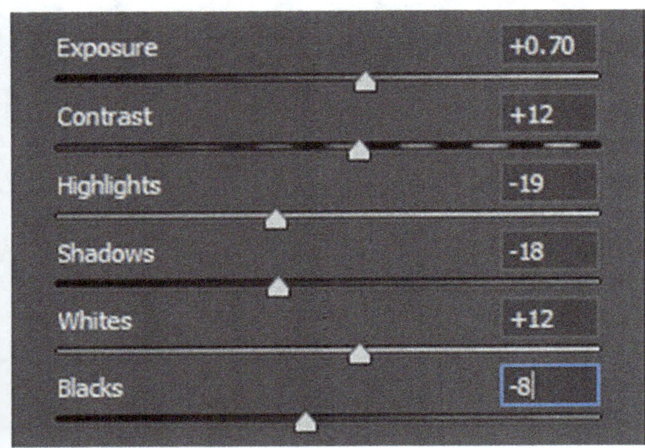

Keep in mind that the 'look' of the photograph will depend on the monitor you are using and whether it is correctly set up or calibrated. For example, if your brightness is turned up quite high on your monitor, your photo will look brighter than it actually is.

Leveling Photos & Removing Lens Distortion

When taking photographs, depending on what lens you use, there is always some kind of distortion. One of the most common issues seen when taking photographs of buildings and architecture, is the angle of walls.

Open **cathedral.jpg** and have a look.

Because the photographer has had to angle the camera upwards to get the whole tower in, the walls are all slanted inwards. Not a very professional looking photo.

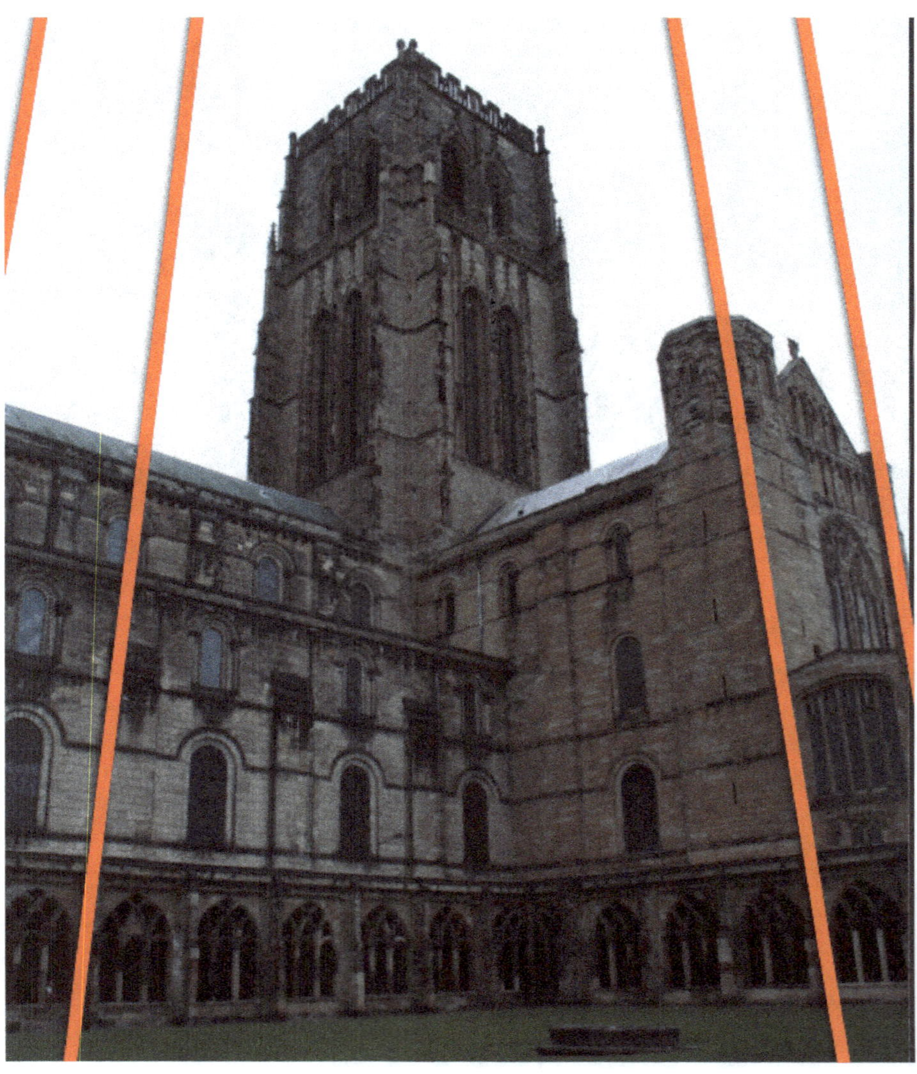

You can use the camera raw filter to remove this distortion. Select the transform tool from the tool bar at the top of the camera raw window.

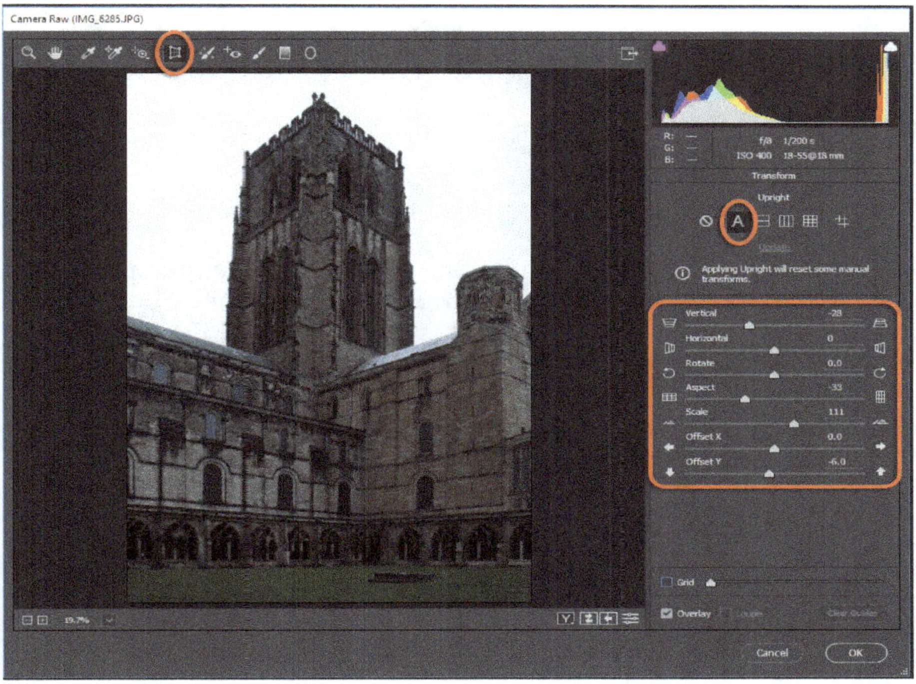

On the right hand side, under the histogram, you'll see some adjustment controls. First, try the auto adjustments along the top, sometimes these do a good enough job. I'm going to try auto first.

It did an ok job but didn't remove the distortion completely. To fine tune the adjustments, underneath you'll see some sliders. The vertical and horizontal controls work well with slanting walls. You will probably also need to enlarge the scale, using the scale slider, as the photo will warp a little bit when applying the corrections. Try them out, see what each slider does. Click OK on the bottom right when you're happy.

Looks a lot better right? You might lose some of the image, but it's a small price to pay for a better looking photograph.

Video Resources

To help you understand the procedures and concepts explored in this book, we have developed some video resources and app demos for you to use, as you work through the book.

As well as the video resources, you'll also find some downloadable files and samples for exercises that appear in the book.

To find the resources, open your web browser and navigate to the following website

`elluminetpress.com/photo`

Do not use a search engine, type the website into the address field at the top of the browser window.

At the beginning of each chapter, you'll find a website that contains the resources for that chapter.

Using the Videos

When you open the link to the video resources, you'll see a thumbnail list at the bottom.

Click on the thumbnail for the particular video you want to watch. Most videos are between 30 and 60 seconds outlining the procedure, others are a bit longer. When the video is playing, hover your mouse over the video and you'll see some controls...

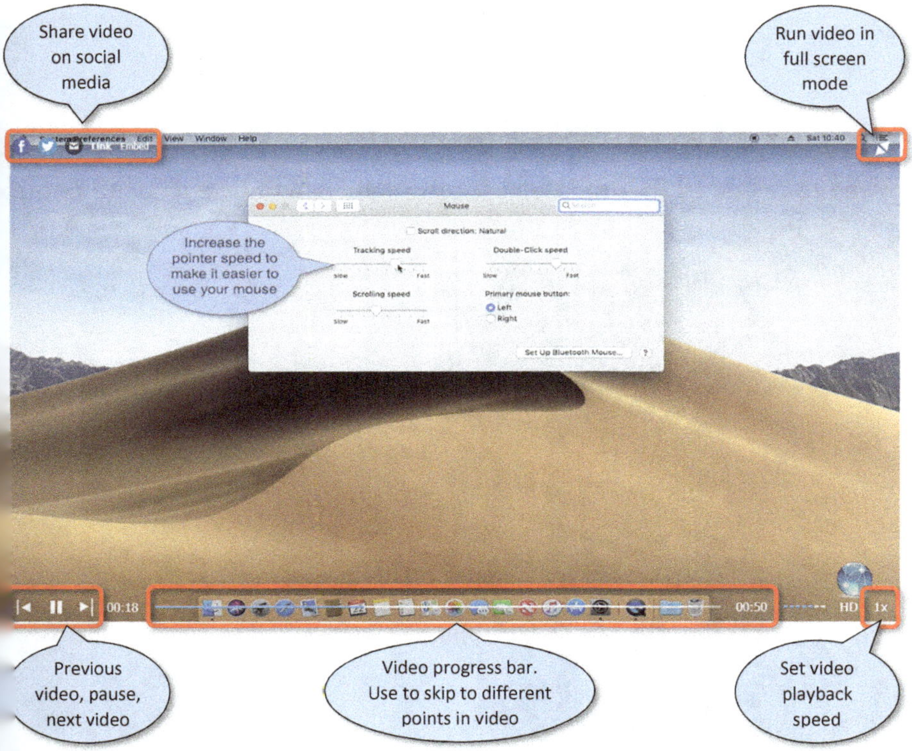

Scanning the Codes

At the beginning of each chapter, you'll a QR code you can scan with your phone to access additional resources, files and videos.

iPhone

To scan the code with your iPhone/iPad, open the camera app.

Frame the code in the middle of the screen. Tap on the website popup at the top.

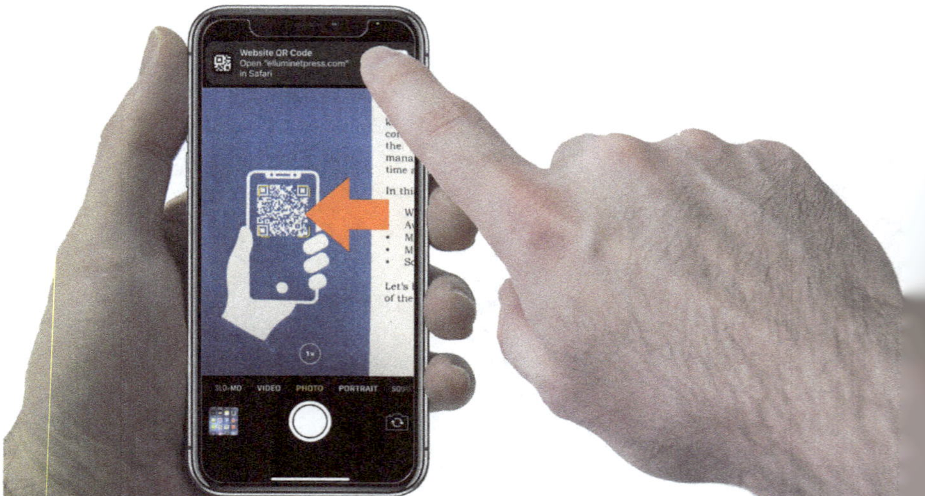

Android

To scan the code with your phone or tablet, open the camera app.

Frame the code in the middle of the screen. Tap on the website popup at the top.

If it doesn't scan, turn on 'Scan QR codes'. To do this, tap the settings icon on the top left. Turn on 'scan QR codes'.

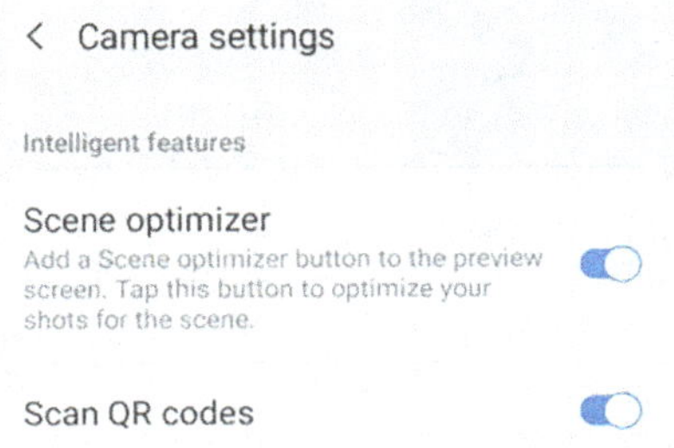

If the setting isn't there, you'll need to download a QR Code scanner. Open the Google Play Store, then search for "QR Code Scanner".

Index

Index

Index

SOMETHING NOT COVERED?

We want to create the best possible resources to help you learn and get things done, so if we've missed anything out, then please get in touch using the links below and let us know. Thanks.

 **office@elluminetpress.com**

 **elluminetpress.com/feedback**